Legal Jams

Cover: a wax impression of the Great Seal of Upper Canada, 1792. Design by Pat Dacey.

Legal Jams

Aspects of Canadian Civil Law

Steven N. Spetz

SIR ISAAC PITMAN (CANADA) LIMITED

SIR ISAAC PITMAN (CANADA) LIMITED
Pitman House, 495 Wellington Street West, Toronto 135, Canada

THE COPP CLARK PUBLISHING COMPANY
517 Wellington Street West, Toronto 135, Canada

SIR ISAAC PITMAN AND SONS LTD.
Pitman House, 39 Parker Street, Kingsway, London, W.C.2
P.O. Box 6038, Portal Street, Nairobi, Kenya

SIR ISAAC PITMAN (AUST.) PTY. LTD.
Pitman House, Bouverie Street, Carlton, Victoria 3053, Australia

PITMAN PUBLISHING COMPANY S.A. LTD.
P.O. Box 9898, Johannesburg, S. Africa

PITMAN PUBLISHING CORPORATION
6 East 43rd Street, New York, N.Y. 10017, U.S.A.

**CONTAINS
RECYCLED
DE-INKED
FIBRE**

The paper used in this book contains approximately 45 percent recycled de-inked fibre. In selecting this paper, we at Pitmans declare our interest in conserving Canada's natural resources and protecting her ecology.

ISBN 0 273 04103 7
Library of Congress Catalog Card Number: 72-80642

Printed and bound in Canada.
1 2 3 4 5 6 7 - 78 77 76 75 74 73 72

Contents

Introduction

Before preparing this text on the subject of legal jams, I had concluded that most people get into more difficulties over contracts than any other branch of law. Excluding criminal offences and torts (such as automobile accidents) the majority of court cases involve contracts. A great deal of material could be compiled about contracts, but this would be voluminous reading and would not necessarily provide the information needed here.

I have attempted in these next pages to centre on common, contemporary problems which people encounter daily and to discuss the law as it pertains to each. New legislation has recently been proposed which could make parts of this text out-dated. Therefore I urge that anyone having a serious legal jam should not rely on the material in this text, but should seek competent legal advice.

The Law and the Poor

Although this text is not written solely for the benefit of poor persons, it may provide some reassurance and useful advice to those who think they are financially unable to provide themselves with legal counsel.

Poor people are more frequently in legal jams than other persons. This is not simply because they haven't the money to pay their bills, but because they are most often victimized. For example, the person residing in a poor neighbourhood often pays more than middle-class persons for the same goods and services. This is easily proved by examining the rents poor families pay for slum apartments. Consequently, low-income families are often anxious to improve their standard of living. Dishonest persons prey upon these motivations to cheat them, usually by tricking them into signing contracts to buy on credit what they cannot afford. Low-income groups are often ill-educated and fall prey to ruses such as pyramid selling which falsely promise to make them money.

Our laws have traditionally reflected the views of the rich, particularly the landed gentry. For example, the *Criminal Code of Canada* makes the penalty for breaking and entering a home life imprisonment. If the person breaking and entering has a weapon, he is also liable to be whipped. This severe penalty reflects the view that a landed person considers his house to be his castle and shows his intense hatred of burglars. On the civil side, our laws have traditionally sided with the creditor against the debtor, the landlord against the tenant, and the seller against the buyer. Until recently, if a tenant did not pay his rent, the landlord seized and sold his personal belongings. A debtor who wouldn't pay a bill because the goods were shoddy might have a sheriff smash down the door, reclaim the goods, and still find himself liable to pay the balance owing. This onesidedness has led to a complete distrust of the law by the poor who view it as the tool by which the rich have cheated them. They often shun courts and hide from bill collectors.

This situation is rapidly changing in Canada. There are several reasons for this optimism. Firstly, new legislation has been passed by Parliament and the provincial legislatures which has greatly helped to remove the inequalities in the law and to provide poor people and consumers with legal strongholds of their own. The exact nature of these laws will be discussed later, but it is enough to say there is a real concern about the problems of the poor and the consumer, and that things are looking up.

Another promising new trend is in the area of legal aid. Traditionally the poor couldn't afford lawyers so they were usually clobbered in court. Or they were easily frightened into submission by a letter from a lawyer threatening to take legal action. They often paid even when they had a legal right not to. Today most people can get legal assistance in some form despite their inability to pay. Most provinces have a legal aid plan. These plans provide legal aid on a free or reduced cost basis, the majority of the cost being paid by the provincial government. In Ontario, a person applies to a regional director stating the nature of his legal problem and his financial situation. If his application is approved, he may go to a lawyer enrolled in the plan and that lawyer will represent him. The lawyer is paid by the government. In some cases, a person is denied legal aid. He can still obtain assistance if he lives near a law school such as Osgoode Hall in Toronto or Queen's University in Kingston. Law students operate their own legal societies and take cases gratis for the practice and because they have a great deal of idealism. How good are they? For the most part, excellent. What they lack in experience they make up for in enthusiasm. Under the direction of law professors, they energetically perform all the legal functions that a lawyer does, except appear in county court or before a Supreme Court. In Ontario they cannot do this until they are members of the Law Society of Upper Canada. However, they can represent a person in a small debts or small claims court. They often win their cases on pencilwork alone. Experienced lawyers lament that the students overwhelm them by their preparation, which they have not done because they have not had the time or because their clients have not been willing to pay them to spend forty hours on a small debts case!

Some provinces have started to set up neighbourhood law offices which are drop-in centres for advice. The advice is free and good, but the lawyers there are donating their time and do not take cases.

In conclusion – the system is not perfect, and probably never will be. The best defence for anyone against a legal jam is awareness and an understanding of the law. Unhappily, not enough people are making an active effort to inform themselves about the law and consequently fall prey to a scheme that uses the law and the courts as a tool to outwit and mistreat those less informed.

Legal Accountability

As a matter of law, some people cannot get into legal difficulties. The reason for this is that they are considered for one reason or another not to be accountable for their actions. The exemption from legal accountability applies particularly to the law of contracts. Generally, those considered unable to contract are:

1. Minors.
2. Insane persons.
3. Intoxicated persons.
4. Indians on reservations.
5. Convicts in penitentiaries.

For the purposes of our discussion, it is perhaps more significant to discuss only the group referred to as minors. Traditionally, a person (male) was considered to be an adult after his twenty-first birthday. For the purposes of contract law, he became an adult at the start of the preceding day. The law does not count part of a day, so his actual birthday does not count. The correct viewpoint is that his twenty-first birthday is the first day of his twenty-second year. Therefore, on the day prior, he actually completes his twenty-first year. This is all rather confusing, but so are other things in law. We might pause a moment and ask where this magic figure of twenty-one came from? Historians believe that at one time a man became a warrior about the age of fourteen. When armour became popular, this age was increased to eighteen because a younger man could not bear the weight of heavy armour. Later the age was raised to twenty-one because the most important legal proceeding in his life, his claim to inheritance and land, required about three years of legal work to become final. This meant that until he had his inheritance he really didn't own anything and couldn't contract for anything. The age of twenty-one as the age of majority evolved – it wasn't established for any specific reason.

This discussion excludes women because it was not until the 20th century that they had any legal status at all.

The movement now is to return to the age of eighteen as that of legal accountability. The United States made recent changes in voting age, etc., and Canada is making full changes in all legal matters to the age of eighteen. Why the need? For one thing, it is felt that persons are mentally able to perform adult functions by the time they pass their eighteenth year. They are often out of school, working, in the armed forces, on police forces, married, and doing many things adults do. It is inconsistent to keep telling them that they are not accountable and are incompetent to contract. In Ontario, the legal age has been set at eighteen for all civil matters. This permits a person over the age of eighteen to vote, consume alcohol, sign contracts, sue and be sued, have his wages garnisheed, and generally engage in all legal activities as an adult and be held fully responsible. Note that the age of eighteen does not have any significance in criminal matters.

There is a certain recognized risk, since eighteen-year olds have often just entered their first job and are eager to make their first major purchases, such as an automobile, furniture, etc. They are somewhat "ripe" for the dishonest merchant to take advantage of. Hopefully, the contents of this text will be a useful guide to both young and old to avoid jams of all kinds.

The young are not the only ones who should be aware of their accountability. Elderly persons, despite their advanced years and perhaps senility, remain responsible for contracts signed even though they may have had little understanding of the terms.

An elderly couple talked with a salesman about having an intercom installed throughout their house. The couple really didn't need such a thing, but the salesman added an interesting sidelight. After the intercom was installed, he would bring other prospective customers to see how it worked. For every sale he made, he would pay the couple fifty dollars. This would afford them a steady income for life, and he would install the intercom at a price 25 percent below market price. The intercom was installed and the company sought to collect the price stated on the contract. The couple's son did some checking and found that his parents had agreed to pay nearly double what the intercom was worth. Not one prospective buyer was brought to the house and there were no fifty-dollar payments. The couple was in financial trouble trying to make payments on the intercom and sought to get out of the entire contract by claiming they had been deceived and didn't really understand all the terms in the contract. They also pointed out that the husband was nearly blind and couldn't read what he signed and that the wife was quite senile and almost in her second childhood. They sought to avoid the contract on the grounds that they were legally not accountable for what they signed. The court could not agree with them. They basically understood the nature of the agreement they were getting in to. It is not an essential point of contract law that both parties understand all the terms. They were not found to be incompetent since they were still living by themselves and were able to care for themselves. Whatever sympathy one might have, this example illustrates that what you sign you must be prepared to be held accountable for.

There is nothing in our law that requires every bargain to be fair, or denies that one person can take advantage of the other. In our free markets, everyone is vulnerable except those specifically declared to be unable to contract. So, for those who have passed their eighteeth birthday and have managed to remain sane, welcome to the world of legal jams.

The Nature of a Contract

Generally, the mere mention of the word contract to a layman fills him with wonder and fear, for he envisions multi-page documents written in strange language and set in tiny print. This description might well be true of many contracts such as insurance policies, but the average person makes more simple than complex contracts in his daily life. These simple contracts need not be written in formal language, in fact they need not be written at all. We can make simple contracts by several methods.

SIMPLE CONTRACTS

Type	Example
Verbal	An oral agreement to take the daily newspaper.
Implied	Ordering a meal in a restaurant implies you will pay for it.
Written	Buying an appliance on the installment plan.

What do all these examples have in common? The answer lies in the definition of a contract:

A contract is an agreement under which both parties assume legal rights and obligations and which is intended to be enforceable at law.

An agreement to meet a friend at four o'clock is not a contract because it is not intended to be enforceable at law (in court). This type of agreement is only a social agreement.

Some contracts are very formal and because of their serious nature they must be in writing, signed in the presence of witnesses who also sign, and then sealed. Seals were originally made of wax, but today they are often red stickers pressed into the paper with a sealer. Or, the letters "L.S." may be used in place of the seal. The derivation of these initials is generally taken to be "locus sigilli" or "place of the seal." These formal contracts are called specialty contracts and include such things as deeds and mortgages.

Many written contracts come to us in unnoticed ways. A ticket to a ball game may have terms printed on the back regarding such things as rain checks, injury to spectators, etc. A store clerk writes out a sales slip with the terms of the sale. Acceptance of the ticket or sales slip may be an implied acceptance of the terms printed on them.

Once a contract is signed, it is generally upheld. However, a person can get out of a contract if there is a formal defect in the contract or the signing, such as:

1. He did not have the legal capacity to sign, e.g., if he were under age.
2. He was forced to sign it against his will.
3. The contract is illegal or contrary to law.
4. The contract is part of a fraudulent scheme.
5. The nature of the agreement has been misrepresented.

A person who has signed a contract does not always remain a party to it. Contracts almost always can be assigned, or transferred to another person for the value they represent, such as payment. This is usually true of anything bought on the installment plan. The retailer assigns his right to collect the money over to a finance company, for which the finance company pays the retailer the amount in full, less a deduction. The debtor is notified that he must now make all payments to the finance company, not the retailer. This is lawful and makes good sense since a finance company is better equipped to collect accounts than a retailer who wants to get his money and buy more stock. Debts cannot be assigned to someone else without the consent of the creditor. Contracts are not intended to be something fearful. We enter into them every day and most are successfully fulfilled. In the next section we take a closer look at special laws which pertain to contracts.

Special Legislation

Some laws have been passed to establish very definite guidelines about contracts. Some are quite recent and modern while others are several hundred years old. Men prepared contracts before the birth of Christ. The Romans used soft clay, then made their impression with a ring that bore the family crest. Later, the clay hardened and made a fairly permanent record. The importance of writing versus spoken word was always recognized. The spoken word is too easily forgotten or changed later. Because of this inherent defect, certain contracts *must* be in writing.

THE STATUTE OF FRAUDS

The Parliament of England first enacted a Statute of Frauds in 1677. This early recognition of the need to curb frauds and perjury in contracts was a landmark in legal history. In Canada, each province has its own version of the statute. Not all the provisions have a bearing on our topic, but generally this law requires certain contracts to *be in writing* if they are to be enforceable. Such contracts include, but are not limited to:

1. A promise to pay the debt, default, or miscarriage of another person. A common example of this is cosigning a note for a friend, which makes the cosigner liable to pay the debt if the friend does not.
2. Contracts for the sale of land or a special right or interest in land. An example of this would be a contract to sell a house and lot, a mortgage, or a grant such as oil or timber rights.
3. Any agreement not to be performed within one year. If a contract is entered into that will last more than a year, or the scheduled date of completion is not intended to be within one year, then it must be in writing.
4. The sale of goods in excess of a certain sum. This will vary from province to province and will be discussed again under The Sale of Goods Act.

It should be noted that provincial statutes of frauds do not prescribe what form a contract must take. Therefore, certain written documents can be called contracts if the terms and the intent of the parties are clear. These include telegrams, letters, memos, notes, of a collection thereof. They are referred to as written memoranda and may constitute contracts.

THE SALE OF GOODS ACT, R.S.O. 1970

Each province legislates special legislation in the field of contracts, especially sales. For the purposes of our discussion, Ontario's statutes will be used, although other provinces have similar legislation. The following are some of the highlights of this Act.

2. – (1) A contract of sale of goods is a contract whereby the seller transfers or agrees to transfer the property in the goods to the buyer for a money consideration called the price, and there may be a contract of sale between one part owner and another.

5. – (1) A contract for the sale of goods of the value of $40 or upwards is not enforceable by action unless the buyer accepts part of the goods so sold and actually receives the same, or gives something in earnest to bind the contract or in part payment or unless some note or memorandum in writing of the contract is made and signed by the party to be charged or his agent in that behalf.

13. In a contract of sale, unless the circumstances of the contract are such as to show a different intention, there is,
(a) an implied condition on the part of the seller that in the case of a sale he has the right to see the goods and that in the case of an agreement to sell he will have a right to sell the goods at the time when the property is to pass;
(b) an implied warranty that the buyer will have and enjoy quiet possession of the goods; and
(c) an implied warranty that the goods will be free from any charge or encumbrance in favour of any third party not declared or known to the buyer either before or at the time when the contract is made.

14. Where there is a contract for the sale of goods by description, there is an implied condition that the goods will correspond with the description and if the sale is by sample as well as by description, it is not sufficient that the bulk of the goods corresponds with the sample if the goods do not also correspond with the description.

17. Where there is a contract for the sale of unascertained goods, no

property in the goods is transferred to the buyer unless and until the goods are ascertained.

38. – (1) Subject to this Act and any statute in that behalf, not withstanding that the property in the goods may have passed to the buyer, the unpaid seller of goods as such has by implication of law,
(a) a lien on the goods or right to retain them for the price while he is in possession of them;
(b) in case of the insolvency of the buyer, a right to stop the goods in transit after he has parted with the possession of them;
(c) a right of resale as limited by this Act.

THE CONDITIONAL SALES ACT, R.S.O. 1970

A contract of sale when full payment for the goods is made immediately is called an absolute sale and The Sale of Goods Act deals with that. Many sales are not made this way. The use of credit, financing, and installment plans has brought about a great increase in the number of conditional sales contracts which are signed. A conditional sales contract is an agreement that permits the buyer to take possession of the goods immediately, use them, and pay for them later. The ownership remains with the seller until the final payment is made. Failure to make payments generally permits the seller to reclaim the goods. The following are some highlights of The Conditional Sales Act in Ontario.

4. The seller shall deliver a copy of the contract to the purchaser within twenty days after the execution thereof, and if, after request, he neglects or refuses to do so the judge of the county or district court in which the purchaser resided when the contract was made may on summary application, make an order for delivery of such copy.

8. – (1) The seller shall, within five days after the receipt of a request in writing from the purchaser of any goods to which this Act applies, or from any other person interested, furnish particulars of the amount remaining due to him and the terms of payment of it, and in default he is guilty of an offence and on summary conviction is liable to a fine of not more than $50.

9. – (1) Where the seller retakes possession of the goods for breach of condition, he shall retain them for twenty days and the purchaser or his successor in interest may redeem the goods within that period on payment of the amount then in arrears, together with interest and the actual costs and expenses of retaking possession.
(2) Where the purchase price of the goods exceeds $30 and the seller intends to look at the purchaser for any deficiency on a resale, the

goods shall not be resold until after a notice in writing of the intention to sell has been given to the purchaser or his successor in interest.

(3) The notice shall contain,

(a) a brief description of the goods;

(b) an itemized statement of the balance of the contract price due and the actual costs and expenses of taking and keeping possession up to the time of the notice;

(c) a demand that the amount as stated in the notice shall be paid over on or before a day mentioned which day shall not be less than twenty days from the day of retaking possession of the goods;

(d) a statement that, unless the amount stated in the notice is paid within the time mentioned, the goods will be sold either at private sale or advertised and sold by public auction, and that the seller intends to look to the purchaser for any deficiency occasioned by any resale.

(4) The notice shall be served personally upon or left at the residence or last known address in Ontario of the purchaser or his successor at least five days before the date set out in the notice for payment or may be sent by registered mail at least seven days before the date set out in the notice for payment addressed to the purchaser or his successor in interest at his last known post office address.

Bills of Exchange Act of Canada 1890

This statute, modelled after a similar act passed in England, defines what are considered to be bills of exchange or negotiable instruments. These terms refer to paper which is used in place of money for conducting business transactions. Included are cheques, promissory notes, and drafts. A bill of exchange is defined as "an unconditional order in writing addressed by one person to another, signed by the person giving it, requiring the person to whom it is addressed to pay on demand or at a fixed or determinable time, a sum certain in money to or to the order of a specified person or to bearer."

Cheque

A cheque is not money or legal tender. It is an order to a bank to pay money out of the drawer's account to the payee (the person to whom the cheque is made out). A person who writes bad cheques, having no money in the bank, commits the criminal offence of obtaining credit by false pretence. If a cheque is accepted as payment, the ownership of goods does not pass until the cheque is honoured by the bank. If it is dishonoured for lack of funds, or payment has been stopped by the drawer, the holder has a right to reclaim his goods or demand valid payment in cash. Cheques may be transferred to another person by endorsing them on the back. There are various types of endorsements, but a full explanation is not necessary for the purposes of our discussion here.

Promissory Notes

A promissory note is an unconditional promise in writing made by one person to another, signed by the maker, engaging to pay on demand or at a fixed or determinable future time, a sum certain in money to or to the order of a specified person, or to bearer. Basically, the note is a promise to pay money which is enforceable solely on the face of the note. No other conditions or provisions need to be proven to enforce collection. Promissory notes are usually signed when a person borrows money or finances an expensive item. Notes can be transferred to another party such as a finance company and can be collected by that finance company without any regard as to why the note was originally given. A new holder is called a "holder in due course" and there are very few defences against paying the note. For example, a man bought an appliance in a store and signed a conditional sales contract and a promissory note to pay for it over twelve months. The store assigned the note to a finance company which began collecting the monthly payments. The appliance stopped working and the store would not honour the guarantee. The angry buyer said he would not make any more payments until the appliance was repaired. Would he have a right to stop making payments?

Traditionally, no. The finance company had every right to receive payments, and had no obligation or interest in what took place between the store and the customer. As an innocent holder in due course, the finance company could collect the payments solely on the face of the note, and any quarrel between the original two parties was none of its concern. This is not the case today. On June 26, 1970, Royal Assent was given to a bill to amend The Bills of Exchange Act which changes in an important way the character of promissory notes given in connection with consumer purchases. The amendment provides that such promissory notes must be prominently and legibly marked on their face with the words "Consumer Purchase." A promissory note so marked is subject to defences or rights of set-off that the purchaser would have had in a claim by the seller. Holders of notes such as finance companies will no longer be able to rely on the status of holder in due course and insulate themselves from disputes between the purchaser and the seller over delivery, performance, service, quality, warranties, or other aspects of the sales contract. This will make it more difficult for unscrupulous vendors to operate, because they will have trouble getting finance companies to take notes off their hands. So, presently, a dissatisfied consumer will have the same rights against whoever holds his note if the item purchased is defective, totally unsatisfactory, or sold under dishonest schemes. The amendment does not apply to notes signed for borrowing money and other purposes, but only to consumer purchases. The provinces have made changes in their Conditional Sales Acts to allow for this amendment to the Federal Act.

This discussion of bills of exchange is not complete, but sufficient for our needs. The reader need only remember the general nature of negotiable instruments during later discussions.

The Consumer Protection Act, R.S.O. 1970

In the early 1960s a rash of books appeared decrying the rate at which the consumer (person who buys and consumes goods) was being cheated at all levels – manufacture, retail, sales. Ralph Nader contended that cars were dangerous and that their makers knew it, and cared not. Being gyped was so commonplace that it was considered part of the normal process of buying goods. The courts were busy collecting debts, seizing property, and running auctions to turn millions of dollars over to dishonest vendors who had hoodwinked someone into signing something they did not understand. The age of plenty had become the age of fraud.

Traditionally, governments seldom interfere with private business transactions. The traditional marketplace has been one where a person was expected to be sharp, and if he got cheated, then he was a little wiser. "Horse-trading" was an art a man could be proud of. What changed so that the government had to intervene? Mainly, what changed was the manner in which goods were sold. The buyer no longer could examine the goods, because they were boxed, sealed in plastic bags, etc., in such a way that he could not open them until he got home. Another problem was the complexity of the items being sold. A buyer could look at a television all day long in a store and wouldn't be able to tell if it was going to work ten years or ten minutes. Consumers began purchasing more and more goods from catalogues instead of actually seeing the goods beforehand, and therefore had to rely on what the catalogue said. New terms became very important – guarantee, money-back, warranty, and other promises that the goods would perform. In many cases, it just didn't happen and the buyer found the seller would do nothing to back up those promises and a finance company was closing in. The poor were still the best target. Unaware of their legal rights, confused by demands to pay interest charges they didn't even know about, frightened by lawyers and collection agencies, they paid and paid, then saw their belongings, even their homes, seized and sold. Enough was enough.

The Consumer Protection Act is not a statute that makes it impossible to get a raw deal. It does not permit anyone who thinks what he agreed to wasn't fair to run to the courts and have the whole thing cancelled. It does not make anyone instantly wiser. What it does is provide minimum guidelines and controls that will hopefully reduce the ease with which people are defrauded and bilked. The following are some of the highlights from that Act..

3. – (1) No person shall carry on business as an itinerant seller unless he is registered under this Act.

N.B. An itinerant seller is a person who does not have a store as such, and sells door to door – the travelling salesman. Because such persons move fast, it was upon them that the greatest anger from shady contracts fell. The buyer who found shoddy goods could not locate the seller who had since left town. Registration requires itinerant sellers to have some sort of address where they can be located, and licenses them to sell in Ontario. The province has the power to remove that licence for dishonest selling.

16. – (1) Every executory contract, other than an executory contract under an agreement for variable credit, shall be in writing and shall contain,
(a) the name and address of the seller and the buyer;
(b) a description of the goods or services sufficient to identify them with certainty;
(c) the itemized price of the goods or services and a detailed statement of the terms of payment;
(d) where credit is extended, a statement of any security for payment under the contract, including the particulars of any negotiable instrument, conditional sale agreement, chattel mortgage or any other security;
(e) where credit is extended, the statement required to be furnished by section 21;
(f) any warranty or guarantee applying to the goods or services and, where there is no warranty or guarantee, a statement to this effect; and
(g) any other matter required by the regulations.
(2) An executory contract is not binding on the buyer unless the contract is made in accordance with this Part and the regulations and is signed by the parties, and a duplicate original copy thereof is in the possession of each of the parties, thereto.

N.B. The terms shown generally require a contract to be complete and state all the terms and conditions. Previous records show that buyers were only given contracts partially completed and that the seller filled in certain items later, such as interest, which the buyer knew nothing about. Often the seller didn't give a copy of the contract to the buyer, but now he must.

18. – (1) Where a seller solicits, negotiates, or arranges for the signing by a buyer of an executory contract at a place other than the seller's permanent place of business, the buyer may rescind the contract by delivering a notice of rescission in writing to the seller within two days after the duplicate original copy of the contract first comes into the possession of the buyer and the buyer is not liable for any damages in respect of such rescission.

(2) Where a buyer rescinds a contract under subsection 1,

(a) the buyer shall immediately return any goods received under the contract and the seller shall bear the expense of the return, not exceeding the expense of returning the goods from the place where the buyer received their delivery; and

(b) the seller shall return any moneys received or realized in respect of the contract, whether from the buyer or any other person, and shall return any trade-in received under the contract.

(3) Where part of the consideration for the sale of goods is a trade-in, the title to the trade-in does not pass to the seller until the two-day period mentioned in subsection 1 has expired without rescission of the contract.

(4) A notice of rescission may be delivered personally or sent by registered mail addressed to the person to whom delivery is required to be made at the address shown in the contract, and delivery by registered mail shall be deemed to have been made at the time of mailing.

N.B. This section is generally termed the "cooling-off" provision. It does not apply to contracts signed in a regular business office, but only to contracts signed in a home or some place other than a regular business office. A person should not be tricked into signing a contract which he is not sure about by a salesman who tells him, "Don't worry, if you change your mind, you have two days to do it. Sign now, and sleep on it. I can't make this special offer again."

20. – (1) Where a buyer under an executory contract has paid two-thirds or more of the purchase price of the goods as fixed by the contract, any provision in the contract or in any security agreement incidental thereto, under which the seller may retake possession of or

resell the goods upon default in payment by the buyer is not enforceable except by leave of a judge of a county or district court.

N.B. This provision is rather significant in that it limits the time when the seller may reposses goods. Imagine the chagrin of a buyer who failed to make his last payment on time and the seller repossessed immediately under the terms of the contract. Now, after two-thirds of the price has been paid, the seller loses his automatic right to repossess and must first get a court order. This does not mean he cannot repossess at all, but that he must take an additional step to do so.

21. Except as provided in section 22, every lender shall furnish to the borrower, before giving the credit, a clear statement in writing showing,
   (a) the sum,
   (i) expressed as one sum in dollars and cents, actually received in cash by the borrower, plus insurance or official fees, if any, actually paid by the lender, or
   (ii) where the lender is a seller, being the amount of the cash price of the goods or services, including any insurance or official fees;
   (b) where the lender is a seller, the sums, if any, actually paid as a down payment or credited in respect of a trade-in, or paid or credited for any reason;
   (c) where the lender is a seller, the amount by which the sum stated under subclause ii of clause *a* exceeds the sum stated under clause *b*;
   (d) the cost of borrowing expressed as one sum in dollars and cents;
   (e) the percentage that the cost of borrowing bears to the sum stated,
   (i) under subclause i of clause *a*, where the lender is not a seller, or
   (ii) under clause *c*, where the lender is a seller,
expressed as an annual rate applied to the unpaid balance thereof from time to time, calculated and expressed in the manner prescribed by the regulations;
   (f) the amount, if any, charged for insurance;
   (g) the amount, if any, charged for official fees; and
   (h) the basis upon which additional charges are to be made in the event of default.

N.B. This section is generally referred to as the disclosure section. Although a reasonably educated person could figure out all these things himself, an alarming number of persons who borrow or buy on credit either could not make such calculations or did not bother. They were unaware of how much interest they were really supposed to pay, what the final total bill was going to be, and that special fees were added on in the form of insurance and other charges. The disclosure at least insures that if a person is interested, he will know all these things before he signs. If he doesn't care, then the law can't do much for him.

The Consumer Protection Act has many other important facets, but they cannot all be explained here. The Act also requires that persons paying on the installment basis receive a statement each payment period clearly showing what they have paid and what they still owe, and the rate of interest they are paying. It is a useful piece of legislation, if for no other reason than to compel creditors to tell the truth to borrowers about what they are going to have to pay. Many never dared show the final figure for fear of scaring the victims away. They preferred only to discuss the monthly figure because this seemed much lower. To most shoppers, the simple $14.95 a month was easier to swallow than $179.40.

The Combines Investigation Act

The Federal Government has a Department of Consumer and Corporate Affairs which has taken an ever-increasing interest in consumer problems. It has established a mail box for any nature of complaint called The Consumer, Box 99, Ottawa. The Department does not guarantee that it will intervene directly in any matter, but is keenly interested in consumer problems so that it can help formulate better legislation. One of the areas which comes directly under this Department is the enforcement of the Combines Investigation Act. This Act is generally aimed against persons who try to fix prices or otherwise violate the principles of free trade. The Act also prohibits false advertising. False advertising is no longer in the Criminal Code of Canada, it was removed and placed in the Combines Investigation Act. The provisions are as follows:

36. – (1) Every one who, for the purpose of promoting the sale or use of an article, makes any materially misleading representation to the public, by any means whatever, concerning the price at which such or like articles have been, are, or will be, ordinarily sold, is guilty of an offence punishable on summary conviction.
(2) Subsection (1) does not apply to a person who publishes an advertisement that he accepts in good faith for publication in the ordinary course of his business.

This Act is presently under review and will probably be replaced by a new Act in 1972 entitled the Competition Act. The Competition Act will go further against unfair practices than any legislation before, and will ban certain practices completely, such as referral selling and pyramid selling. The Director of the Combines Investigation Branch may investigate any retailer or other seller whom he believes is engaging in any form of misleading advertising, and award fines and possibly refer the matter to court for more stringent punishment.

A 3 0 6 8

Conditions, Warranties, Guarantees

The legal differences between conditions and warranties or guarantees are important to note as are the legal effects of each of these promises.

A condition is a term added to a contract that is so significant that failure to meet the condition is a complete failure to carry out the contract. The buyer has the right to rescind the entire contract and recover any loss suffered. For example, a buyer agreed to buy a camper on the condition that the seller would make repairs and alterations that would make the camper safer on the road. When the buyer returned to pick up the camper, none of the work had been done. The buyer is excused from completing the sale, because a fundamental condition of the contract was not met – making alterations.

Guarantees and warranties are basically the same thing, and are quite different from conditions. A warranty is only in addition to the contract and is not a fundamental part of it. Failure to live up to a guarantee or warranty does not permit the buyer to rescind the contract, but only to a certain adjustment in the contract according to the terms of the warranty. Nearly every major product on the market today comes with a warranty of some type. Most cars have warranties on nearly every item for one year, plus a five-year or 50,000-mile warranty on drive components. Many buyers are much influenced by warranties in deciding what to buy, but are warranties really so important and are they legally enforceable?

Most manufacturers are not giving anything away when they paste or tie warranties onto their products. The warranty is usually worded so strangely that no one, lawyer or consumer, can really understand it, let alone try to enforce it. Automobile manufacturers often print the warranty, then print a "translation" of the warranty explaining it. Here are some excerpts from a warranty on a large, brand-name electric range.

"X" Company warrants to the purchaser of each new electric range that any part thereof, which proves to be defective in material or

workmanship under normal domestic use within one year from the date of original purchase for use, will be repaired or replaced without charge. It is understood that the customer will pay for such labour as is required to replace said inoperative parts.

This warranty will not apply if in the judgement of the company, damage or failure has resulted from accident, alteration, misuse, abuse, or operation on an incorrect power supply.

Note that the manufacturer retains the final decision as to whether or not the product is defective, or has been misused. Note that labour costs of a bum product must still be borne by the customer, even if the range was defective from the time it left the factory. This means the customer is without use for a period of time, and has to pay the labour costs of having the range rebuilt – because it wasn't built right the first time.

Are warranties totally worthless? Experts say no, they are worth having, *if* they will be honoured. Therefore, it is the dealer who really counts, not the warranty. This can be boiled down into a saying worth remembering: "A warranty is only as good as the man behind it." If the dealer is a reputable businessman, he will attempt to honour all warranties because he has a stake in the community and in his reputation. A fly-by-night dealer has no such stake and will renege on the warranty every time. One consumer bought a used car and it was a lemon. When he asked about the guarantee the dealer gave him, he got the reply, "Guarantee? Sure I guarantee the car – it's a car, that's what I guarantee."

At the present time, there is very little a person can do about a warranty that is not honoured. If the wording of the warranty seems quite definite, it might be worth a law suit against the person who gave it. The proposed replacement to the Combines Investigation Act, the Competition Act, contains a special provision to make warranties much more enforceable. When this new legislation is passed, and if it is passed in its present form, warranties will take on a new, more significant meaning than they presently hold.

Borrowing Money

Many people borrow money at some point in their lives, and often for a very sensible reason. Our financial institutions are thriving, as credit becomes more and more recognized as a means to make financial transactions. There are various sources of borrowing money, and several of these will be discussed here.

BANKS AND TRUST COMPANIES

Banks and trust companies make loans for various reasons. Trust companies prefer mortgages while the banks take a more active interest in consumer loans for automobiles, holidays, etc. Both require security for most loans, in the form of collateral such as real estate, bonds, etc., which guarantees that the loan will be repaid. Let's examine the legal aspects of a mortage just momentarily. A mortgage is a loan for which the borrower gives back as security the property itself. Payments are made monthly for a set period, such as twenty years, until the mortgage is paid. Interest is part of every payment, being very much front-end loaded during the first years. In reality, the first payments are almost pure interest and the property owner gains very little towards paying off his debt. His debt is eliminated by a system called amortization, which calculates the interest first, then credits the remainder towards the principal. For example, a man with a $20,000 mortgage on his house at 9 percent makes monthly payments of $173.60. From the first payment, $150.00 is extracted in interest; $23.60 is actually paid on the house. Each subsequent payment contains less interest and more principal and as the years progress he is making much better headway. However, if he sells the house within two or three years after buying it, he will be dismayed to find out that he has paid off practically none of it. Another important legal aspect of a mortgage is that the borrower promises personally to pay the mortgage as well as provide collateral. This is his "personal covenant" and he is bound to it even if he sells the house to someone else and that someone is supposed to take over the mortgage. The best way to sell a mortgaged house is to make the buyer get his own mortgage and pay your mortgage off completely.

Loans for consumer goods such as cars are more popular with banks than trust companies. Banks require collateral for most loans and charge considerable more interest for unsecured loans. At one time, the Bank Act prohibited banks from charging more than 6 percent interest. This restriction was removed in 1967 and banks can now charge rates competitive with other institutions. The Concumer Protection Act requires that banks show the true cost of borrowing as an annual percentage figure, as well as in dollars and cents. An example follows:

Amount borrowed: $500.00
Cost of borrowing: ....$ 87.75
Amount to be repaid: $587.75
1st payment: ....$ 16.20
Remaining payments: ....$ 16.33
Number of payments: 36
True annual interest rate: 10.82%

FINANCE COMPANIES

A finance company is one of the few lending institutions that is still prohibited from charging beyond a certain rate of interest. On small loans, this limit is as follows:

2% per month on the first $300
1% per month on the next $700
½% per month on the next $500

Where a loan of $500 or less is made for a period greater than 20 months or exceeding $500 for more than 30 months, the cost of the loan shall not exceed 1 percent per month on the unpaid balance.

This means that a person who borrowed $1200 from a finance company could be asked to pay interest for the first month as follows:

First $300 @   2% = $6.00
Next $700 @   1% =   7.00
Next $200 @ ½% =   1.00
                    ─────────
                    $14.00 interest

This is a rather high interest rate, and the reader might ask why it is permitted to be so high. The reasons are several and quite legitimate. On small loans, the cost of bookkeeping is rather high in terms of the amount borrowed. The number of loans which are bad debts and require legal action is rather high. Finance companies lend money to persons other institutions turned down, usually because of lack of collateral. They are taking greater risks and can charge more interest.

TRUE ANNUAL INTEREST RATE

When a loan is taken out, the lender must show the borrower the true annual interest rate. This is calculated using a very long formula, but a short formula gives an answer that is *almost* accurate. If a person borrowed $600 and agreed to pay it back at the rate of $50 a month plus interest of $3 a month, or $53 a month for 12 months, he might conclude that he would pay $36 interest for the loan of $600 or roughly 6 percent. This sort of calculation is not accurate, because as the loan is paid off, the interest should decrease rather than remain a $3 a month. The formula for true annual interest will show a different answer.

$$i = \frac{2 \times P \times C}{A (n + 1)}$$

i = True annual interest
P = Payments per year
C = Interest charge in dollars (total)
A = Amount borrowed
n = Number of payments in entire contract

Solution:

$$i = \frac{2 \times 12 \times \$36}{\$500 (12 + 1)}$$

$$i = \frac{\$864}{\$6500} = 13.3\% \text{ interest}$$

OTHER SOURCES FOR BORROWING MONEY

Cash can be obtained from the cash surrender value of a life insurance policy at the given interest rate stated in the policy. That is, a whole life policy with a cash surrender value of $3,000 may provide up to that amount as a loan at the stated rate, such as 7 percent. The borrower should note that the amount of the loan is deducted from the face value of the policy until it is repaid. A $20,000 policy against which a $3,000 loan is outstanding will only pay $17,000 if the holder dies.

Credit unions lend money at fairly low interest rates and provide excellent service to those who otherwise couldn't get credit. Collateral is not often requested, and fewer personal questions are asked, as well. A loan which exceeds the lawful interest rates is deemed to be exorbitant and cannot be collected. Charging an unlawful rate of interest is called usury and is punishable by fines under the various acts regulating the charging of interest. If a person borrows money from a private source, there is no set rate of interest that may be charged, but the court will not allow a rate so high as to be exorbitant.

Credit Bureaus and Collection Agencies

The popularity of credit has brought about a need for some sort of central information centre that keeps track of users and abusers of credit. In order to provide a merchant or lending institution with a rating for a prospective credit customer, credit bureaus have sprung up all over Canada and the United States. These private companies keep a file on every individual in the community who has ever borrowed money in any form. Stores and lending institutions have a membership with the credit bureau for which they pay an annual fee. They also pay a small fee for each referral they make to the bureau. In practice it works something like this: A store wants to know if a customer is a good risk for buying something on the installment plan. The store calls the bureau and gives a code number over the phone. This number establishes that the caller is a member of the bureau and entitled to information. The caller then gives the full name of the customer and the bureau makes a check of its records to establish what kind of risk the person would be, based on his past record. If he is a prompt-paying type, the reply is a good one – let's say 0-1 which means the bureau has no derogatory information about him. Based on this rating, the store may go ahead and grant credit. If the bureau finds that the name given matches one in their files who has been a slow payer, but not a really bad risk, the rating may be 0-4, and the store must decide if it wants to take a chance. A rating such as 0-9 represents a credit-bankrupt person who should not receive any further credit. The bureau does not make the decision to grant credit, but only recommends to the store what should be done. If a person suspects he is getting a bad rating from a credit bureau, he can do very little about it legally, but most bureaus are willing to talk it over and make suggestions as to how a credit rating can be improved. At the time of writing, there is a proposed Bill before Parliament to make it mandatory for credit bureaus to permit the public to see what they have on file so they can argue if something is wrongly entered under their name, and this can happen.

Collection agencies are altogether different than credit bureaus. The collection agency does a thriving business in our debt-ridden world. What are its legal powers?

A careful distinction should be made between collection agencies and finance companies. Collection agencies do not lend money, and therefore do not obtain notes first-hand from business. They collect money for other people, generally business firms, banks, professional people, even the government. Their actions are governed by The Collection Agencies Act of Ontario, R.S.O. 1970.

A person who has money owed to him and cannot collect it, engages the services of the collection agency. Where court action is taken by a collection agency, it is usually the debtor who pays the costs. If the account is to be taken to the Small Claims court, which handles claims up to $400.00, the court clerk has to summon the debtor by registered letter, the standard fee for this being $3.60. If the court bailiff has to deliver the summons in person, as he is required to do if the amount is over $35.00, the mileage charge is 20¢ a mile, one way. If the debtor is not at home and the bailiff has to return, that means another 20¢ a mile.

Where court action is initiated by a collection agency, the agency has to advance court costs, another $4.00 to $12.00 depending on the amount involved. In this case, the court costs will be passed along as a charge to the client firm. The first money paid by the debtor to the collection agency will allow the agency to get its money back. The firm will be left to deal with the customer.

Collection methods seem rather uniform. First a letter goes to the debtor telling him that the account is now in the hands of the agency and the debtor is expected to pay them rather than the firm where the bill was contracted. The letter usually suggests the debtor come into the office in order to protect his good name and credit rating. If there is no response to the letter, a phone call usually follows. The Collection Agencies Act of Ontario clearly prohibits threatening or abusive phone calls.

When the phone call fails, the next stage is a warning called an "intention to summons" which gives the debtor forty-eight hours to make some agreement before the matter goes to court.

The agency cannot take the case to court without the creditor's consent, but if this is given the agency may file suit the next day. Most agencies have to take 50 percent of their cases to court. The others settle sooner. At any time, a small claims court clerk may have 3,000 or more such cases pending, most of which will be settled in court.

A person pressed by a collection agency should see a lawyer without delay if he feels the debt is unjust. If he has no money, he should seek legal aid. Under no circumstances should the debtor ignore the matter or fail to appear if summonsed. The normal procedure is for the court to order collection through garnishee – an order to the debtor's employer to deduct 30 percent of his wages each pay day until the debt is paid. If the debtor is not working, other things can be garnisheed such as bank accounts, etc. Remember, added to the debt are the costs, bailiff's expenses, legal fees, etc.

Landlord and Tenant

A relationship over property in which the owner rents the use of the property to another person is called a landlord and tenant relationship. Such agreements are very old and traditionally involved renting land to a person to grow crops. A feudal landlord owned large tracts of land, usually because they were given to him by the monarch. He could not farm all the land himself, so he divided it into plots and rented it to farmers who would plant and harvest crops. The landlord received part of the crops or the proceeds from them as rent and the tenants kept the rest. The landlord had no obligation to the tenant at all, the only obligations were from the tenant to the landlord. The landlord could evict the tenant at any time for any reason. There was no understanding that the landlord would provide a house, the tenant had to construct his own. If the tenant were evicted, the house remained the property of the landlord since he owned the land it rested upon.

This relationship is seldom in force today, since tenant farmers are few. What has taken its place is a new relationship, one of living accommodations. The landlord provides a house or apartment and the tenant pays rent in cash, not in some form of produce. The responsibilities of landlord and tenant are not the same, since the type of agreement is radically different.

Traditionally, the landlord has had most of the rights. Any violation on the part of the tenant has meant eviction and landlords have had powerful allies in court which would allow them to charge in and seize just about everything the tenant owned to pay for rent, damages, etc. On the other hand, the tenant could do little if the place was a fire trap, leaked, or had no heat. It was his choice to like it or leave.

The Landlord and Tenant Act of Ontario typified this lack of concern for the tenant until it was revised in 1970 regarding residential leases. This section will be mostly devoted to a discussion of the changes which the revised Act brought into being.

31

LEASES

The lease agreement is the rental contract between the landlord and tenant. It may be written or it may be verbal, in certain cases. A verbal lease is valid only after the tenant has moved in. For example, if a landlord and tenant agreed verbally to establish a lease under which the tenant would pay rent of $130 a month, and the lease was on a month to month basis, then this agreement becomes binding on both parties after the tenant has taken over the premises, not before.

However, most parties prefer a written or printed lease. There are various lease forms that can be purchased for both houses and apartments. Appartment leases are quite long and cannot be reproduced here in total, but some of the major items that are usually contained are included. The tenant should read and understand his lease before entering into it. If he can't understand it, he should have competent legal counsel explain it – not the landlord who may have his own version. The following questions should be very clear in his mind:

1. For what term is the lease?
The tenant should be clear as to how long he is agreeing to rent the premises. Yearly? Month to month? If the original term runs out, must a new lease be signed or is there an automatic renewal clause? Some leases state that the first term is one year, then the lease automatically reverts to a month to month lease. If nothing is provided, then it is assumed that when the original lease runs out it is renewed under the same conditions as before. For example, if a one-year lease ran out with neither party saying anything about renewal, another yearly lease is assumed to exist.

2. How can I terminate the lease if I wish?
When you enter any agreement, always know where the door is. What does the lease say about moving out, etc.? In the absence of any exact provisions, The Landlord and Tenant Act will apply as is discussed later regarding giving notice.

3. When and how must I pay rent?
The lease should state if rent is due in advance or at the end of the month or lease period. If cheques are not specified as acceptable, clarify whether the landlord will accept cheques.

4. What are the rules of rental?

Clarify everything regarding pets, how many people may reside, sub-leasing, noise, parties, etc. If it is not stated in the lease, write it in and have the landlord initial the change to indicate that he agreed to it.

5. What are my obligations?

The lease should state under what circumstances the tenant agrees to repair things. He is not usually responsible for wear and tear, or damage by storms or repainting the outside, etc. But he is required to fix anything he breaks, including locks, windows, etc.

6. What are the landlord's obligations?

Clarify such questions as heat, major repairs, repairs to appliances that are built-in if they stop working. Don't rely on verbal promises by the landlord that he will fix anything and everything, especially things that aren't working when you move in. Insure that it is written in the lease.

IMPORTANT CHANGES IN THE LANDLORD AND TENANT ACT 1970

Damage Deposits

Until 1970, it was common practice for landlords to demand from each tenant a sum of money to be held as a guarantee that the tenant would not damage something on the premises and refuse to repair it or leave the premises in a state of uncleanliness which would require the landlord to undergo major cleaning or redecorating. This sum was called a damage deposit and the landlord would return the entire amount if the premises were well kept. This was a reasonable theory, but tenants objected to it. Why? The chief reason was abuse by some landlords who were dishonest. They refused to repay any damage deposits to anyone, regardless of how well kept the premises were. This sum might be $50 to $100 and in an apartment house where many tenants came and went, the profits were rather substantial. The landlord would just claim that damages occurred which did not occur, but how could the tenant prove anything in court? Some landlords charged every tenant for the same scratches on woodwork, etc.

The tenant could try to get his deposit back by suing but this usually cost more than it was worth. The revised act makes damage deposits unlawful and landlords are prohibited from collecting them.

Advance Rent

On the other side of the coin, landlords can point out tenants who got several months behind in rent then skipped town one night. The landlord would be out several hundred dollars and could do little about it. The revised Act sympathized with honest landlords and recognized that all tenants are not reliable. The Act permits landlords to collect two months rent for the first month. The rent is considered to be the first month's rent and the last month's rent. The landlord has been paid in advance for the last month, so when the tenant gives notice that he is leaving, he does not pay the last month's rent. This gives the landlord some protection against tenants who skip town. If they have already paid one month in advance, the chances are they aren't going to beat the landlord out of more than a few weeks' rent, if he keeps tabs on them.

Distress

The traditional meaning of distress was that if a tenant did not pay his rent, the landlord could seize his personal goods and have them sold at auction. The sheriff's office was usually called upon to do the honours, and the tenant was virtually a prisoner until enough of his furniture, clothing, etc. were sold to pay the rent. Then, he was ignominiously kicked out. This unpleasant scene of breaking down doors, grabbing someone's personal and sometimes very sentimental belongings and selling them was rather deplorable. While one might sympathize with a landlord who is unpaid, the solution was too harsh. The right of distress was entirely abolished under the revised Act. A landlord must sue in court for unpaid rent, just as any creditor must sue when a bill is not paid. His only defence is the one months' rent he collected in advance.

Terminating the Lease by Tenant

Like many agreements, if the landlord does not live up to his part of the bargain, the tenant may terminate the lease even if it has not expired. Normal termination, though, takes place at the end of the lease period. Advance notice depends on the length of the lease.

GIVING NOTICE

Lease Period	Notice Required
Weekly	A notice to terminate a weekly tenancy must be given on or before the last day of the following week of the tenancy. Weekly does not mean Sunday to Saturday, but seven days.
Monthly	A notice to terminate a monthly lease shall be given on or before the last day of one month of the tenancy to be effective on the last day of the following month of the tenancy. Monthly does not mean a calendar month, but the same date of the month preceding.
Yearly	A notice to terminate a year to year tenancy shall be given on or before the sixtieth day before the last day of any year of the tenancy to be effective on the last day of that year of the tenancy. Yearly does not mean calendar year, January to December, but a time period of 365 days.

The chief difference between wording of the old and the revised Act is the deletion of the reference to calendar weeks, months, or years. This used to mean that an entire month from the first day to the last had to be included in the notice period. If a tenant had a lease that expired on May 15, he would have to give his notice before the last day of March. This was because one clear calendar month was required, i.e., all of April. Now, he must only give one month, which would be any time prior to April 15.

Termination of Lease by Landlord
A landlord can require a tenant to leave under various conditions, as explained below.

1. End of lease.
When the lease runs out, there is no obligation on the part of the landlord to renew it. He can inform the tenant that the lease has expired and that he will not renew and the tenant must leave. He does not have to prove any misconduct on the part of the tenant.

2. Failure to pay rent.

If the tenant does not pay rent on the required dates, this is a breach of the lease and the landlord may evict the tenant, using the same time periods of notice as shown in the chart. The landlord is under no obligation to accept late payment.

3. Violation of lease terms.

If the tenant does not comply with the lease terms, he can be evicted. Defaulting includes offences such as having pets, making noise, ignoring needed repairs, etc. The notice to vacate need not be in a particular form, but the following words are generally used.

NOTICE TO TENANT

To ....

(Name of Tenant)

I hereby give you notice to deliver up possession of the premises

....

(identify the premises)

which you hold of me as tenant, on the .... day of ....
next, or on the last day of the period of your tenancy next following the giving of this notice.

Dated this .... day of ...., 19 ....

....

(Landlord)

The proper way for the landlord to serve notice is to personally give it to the tenant. If the tenant evades or refuses to take the notice, the landlord may serve it on him by giving it to another responsible adult upon the premises who resides with the tenant, posting it up in a conspicuous place upon some part of the premises, or by sending it to him by registered mail. If the tenant still refuses to leave, he is considered an overholding tenant and can be responsible for rent and other damages the landlord may suffer. At this point the landlord cannot throw him out, but may apply for a court order of eviction (writ of possession) from a county or district court judge, which can be carried out by the sheriff's office.

Repairs

In addition to the terms of the lease, The Landlord and Tenant Act puts some minimum requirements on both landlord and tenant regarding repairs. Traditionally, the landlord was not required to keep unfurnished premises in good repair and could rent out any fallen down slum imaginable, unless the Department of Health ordered it closed. Now, this is not quite the case.

> 95. – (1) A landlord is responsible for providing and maintaining the rented premises in a good state of repair and fit for habitation during the tenancy and for complying with health and safety standards, including any housing standards required by law, and notwithstanding that any state of nonrepair existed to the knowledge of the tenant before the tenancy agreement was entered into.
>
> (2) The tenant is responsible for ordinary cleanliness of the rented premises and for the repair of damage caused by his wilful or negligent conduct or that of persons who are permitted on the premises by him.
>
> (3) The obligations imposed under this section may be enforced by summary application to a judge of the county or district court of the county or district in which the premises are situate and the judge may,
>
> (a) terminate the tenancy subject to such relief against forfeiture as the judge sees fit;
>
> (b) authorize any repair that has been or is to be made and order the cost thereof to be paid by the person responsible to make the repair, such cost to be recovered by due process or by set-off;
>
> (c) make such further or other order as the judge considers appropriate.
>
> (4) This section applies to tenancies under tenancy agreements entered into or renewed after this section comes into force and to periodic tenancies on the first anniversary date of such tenancies after this section comes into force and in all other cases the law applies as it existed immediately before this section comes into force.

Our discussion of the landlord and tenant agreement is not complete, but has attempted to illustrate some of the matters which most often involve landlord and tenant in a legal jam.

The Employment Standards Act, R.S.O. 1970

Labour relations are an area of provincial responsibility. Different provinces have enacted various statutes to regulate employment practices. In 1968 Ontario established the Employment Standards Act to combine various bits of legislation into one Act administered by the Ontario Department of Labour. The main features of this Act are explained here.

HOURS OF WORK

The Act requires that the working hours of an employee shall not exceed eight in the day and forty-eight in the week. An employee is one who works for another person and is paid by that person, but does not include management officials or those salaried annually. Such persons are expected to devote whatever amount of time is necessary to accomplish their responsibilities. Where the need for extra hours is established because of the nature of the work or where emergency situations arise, the employer may apply for an overtime permit from the Ontario Department of Labour. With certain exceptions, the excess number of working hours must not exceed 100 hours a year.

A girl under eighteen must not work more than six hours overtime in a week, or fifty-four total hours in a week.

OVERTIME PAY

The Act provides that an employee will receive a minimum of one and a half times his regular wage rate for work performed in excess of forty-eight hours a week. This provision is designed to discourage the use of excessive overtime as well as to ensure that workers, particularly those in low-wage or seasonal industries who must work long hours to improve their earnings, will receive a premium rate for overtime.

Special overtime provisions have been established for certain industries and details can be obtained from the Employment Standards Branch of the Department of Labour.

PREMIUM PAY FOR HOLIDAYS WORKED

Where an employee works on any of the seven statutory holidays set out in the Act (New Year's Day, Good Friday, Victoria Day, Dominion Day, Labour Day, Thanksgiving Day, and Christmas Day) he must receive one and a half times his regular wage rate unless substitute holidays are arranged with the approval of the Director of the Employment Standards Branch.

MINIMUM WAGES

Minimum wages were first introduced in Ontario in 1920. Under the Employment Standards Act, the minimum wage rate for general industry has been raised from $1 an hour to $1.30; in the construction industry the rate has gone up to $1.55 an hour. These rates are subject to constant change and may be higher upon reading. The purpose of the minimum wage is to provide protection for workers who are open to exploitation and who have little or no bargaining power. It also acts to place a floor under wages in order to guard against unfair competition between employers based on low wages. Special wage rates have been established for students and seasonal workers. The general student rate is $1 an hour. A fruit and vegetable processor receives $1.30 an hour. Resorts must pay summer help $1.15 an hour. Again, these rates are subject to change, and the most current rates can be obtained from the Ontario Department of Labour, Employment Standards Branch.

Industries under federal government jurisdiction, such as banks, airlines, and railways, are not convered by this Act but come under the Canada Labour Standards Code.

EQUAL PAY FOR EQUAL WORK

Women now represent an important and growing proportion of the work force. To protect their rights, the former provisions dealing with equal pay for equal work which were part of the Human Rights Code of Ontario, have been transferred to the Department of Labour, Employment Standards Branch. It now provides that men and women doing the same work in the same establishment must get the same pay. The definition of same work is determined on the basis of equal skill, effort, and responsibility, under similar work conditions.

VACATIONS WITH PAY

A paid holiday is an annual vacation which the employer must bear the cost of for the benefit of his employees. Union contracts have been very successful in obtaining such benefits, but nonunion workers would be without this benefit if the government did not insure it for them as well. The Employment Standards Act provides that every employee shall be given an annual vacation of at least one week on completion of each twelve months' employment. Teachers and seasonal workers are not included. The vacation pay must be not less than 2 percent of the total pay received in the year for which the vacation is given. Whether he works for a day, a week, or a month, every worker must receive vacation pay at the rate of 2 percent of his total pay for the period of employment. After three years of employment, the minimum standard is two weeks paid vacation and vacation pay of not less than 4 percent of annual earnings. There is not included in the Act a provision that the employee must take the vacation. If he wants to work fifty-two weeks a year, he then receives his vacation pay as a bonus. This money is taxable on his income tax return.

WAGE REPORTING

Employers are required to furnish every employee with a statement at the time wages are paid. In addition to the net sum, the statement must show the employee's wage rate and the period of time for which the wages are being paid, the wage entitlement, the amount of all deductions and allowances and the purpose of each.

Deductions include those authorized by the employee as well as unemployment insurance, income tax, Canada pension, company pension plan and hospitalization insurance.

COLLECTION OF UNPAID WAGES

The Department of Labour may now collect unpaid wages for an employee, including the amount of wages due, overtime, and vacation pay, up to a maximum of $1,000. Formerly, collection on behalf of an employee could be made only for wages up to the level of the minimum rate.

ENFORCEMENT

The Department of Labour has the authority to make audits and call for information in administering and enforcing the Act. The legislation provides for penalties in the form of fines, up to a maximum of $1,000 which may be imposed on employers found guilty of contravening the regulations or failing to comply with directions issued.

EMPLOYMENT OF FEMALES

No female employee under the age of eighteen may work in an establishment between the hours of twelve o'clock midnight and six o'clock in the morning. Where the work period of a female employee ends between midnight and six o'clock, the employer must provide her with private transportation to her residence at his expense. Where the work period of a female begins between midnight and six o'clock, the employer must provide her with private transportation from her residence to the place of employment at his expense.

Civil Court Procedures and Remedies

Civil cases are generally referred to a particular court because of the amount of money involved. Each province establishes its own civil courts, and the names vary somewhat from province to province. Again, Ontario will be our example.

SMALL CLAIMS COURT

The lowest civil court is Small Claims Court. Each county is divided into a number of divisions according to need by population. The limit for a single case is not more than $400. If the court is in a district instead of a county, the limit is $800. The court is staffed by a professional judge, although in some areas lawyers have been temporarily appointed to the bench. The procedures are less formal in order to handle many small cases rapidly. It is permissible to represent yourself in this court and not hire a lawyer since the amount claimed is often so small that paying a lawyer would be more costly than it's worth. Or you may represent someone else and act as their agent. The payment of a small court fee covers all the necessary documents and the cost of collecting from the debtor.

A plaintiff commences an action in small claims court by filing his claim in writing with the clerk of the proper court. (The first thing that must be determined in this case is which division the plaintiff lives in, and which division the debtor lives in.) A summons is served on the defendant telling him he has ten days to file a defence. If he does not file, a judgement will be entered against him by default. If the defendant files a defence, called a dispute, the clerk sends a copy of it to the plaintiff or to his lawyer, together with a notice of trial. A notice of trial is also sent to the defendant. The court fees are chargeable to the plaintiff immediately upon filing. For a very small claim, the fee can be as little as four dollars. Rarely does it exceed fifteen dollars unless the plaintiff also wants to summons witnesses, or request a jury trial.

Most cases in Small Claims Court are undefended since the usual type of claim is for unpaid bills to which there is no valid defence. Other cases are defended, and judgement is awarded based on the merits of the case. What happens then? The judge gives judgement to one party or the other. Assuming the plaintiff wins, he may ask for various remedies:

1. Garnishee – If the defendant has a known occupation, the judge may send a court order to his employer directing the employer to deduct part of his wages until the debt is paid.

2. Attachment – The debtor's bank accounts, safety deposit box, real estate, and other investments may be attached by court order, meaning these things are inaccessible to him until the debt is paid. The judge can order the debtor to reveal in court all the assets he owns.

3. Driving Privileges – If the debt arose from a motor vehicle accident, the debtor's vehicle permit and driver's licence may be suspended until the judgement is paid.

4. Contempt of Court – Where the debtor is able to pay, but won't, he can be found in contempt of court and sentenced to jail for a period not exceeding forty days. If a person is penniless, he is not jailed since his failure to pay was not wilful, but something he was powerless to do.

COUNTY COURT

The next highest court is the County Court. It hears civil cases where the sum involved does not exceed $7,000 and cases over this amount where both sides agree to be heard. The procedure is more formal than in Small Claims Court and each party must be represented by a lawyer. A case may be tried by judge, or by judge and jury. In libel or slander cases, a jury is always called and is usually called in negligence cases, since it must determine the extent of damages. In cases of technical complexity, a jury is not called, since it would not understand the issues. If either party wishes a jury, he sends a jury notice to the other party. If that party does not wish a jury, he petitions a judge to strike out the jury notice. The judge then makes the final determination. A civil jury in Ontario consists of six persons, five of whom must agree to reach a verdict. The damages are a separate matter, and failing to reach a decision as to the amount of damages does not necessarily mean a hung jury; the judge may adjudicate the matter.

HIGH COURT, ONTARIO SUPREME COURT, TRIALS DIVISION

This court hears civil matters involving more than $7,000, as well as certain criminal cases. This court would also hear a claim against the provincial government.

HIGH COURT, ONTARIO SUPREME COURT, APPEALS DIVISION

This branch of the Supreme Court hears appeals from the trials division of the same court and from lower courts.

FEDERAL COURT OF CANADA

This newly created court hears cases involving a direct claim against the departments of the federal government. It has replaced a variety of previous federal courts, including the Court of Exchequer. It also has jurisdiction over appeals made against rulings by federal regulatory agencies such as the C.R.T.C. (Canadian Radio and Television Commission). Like the provincial supreme courts, it has two branches, a trials division and an appeals division.

SUPREME COURT OF CANADA

A civil case involving more than $10,000 may be appealed to the highest court of Canada, the Supreme Court. With the creation of the new Federal Court of Canada, the number of cases in the Supreme Court is expected to be reduced, so that it can concentrate on cases of social significance and constitutional questions which concern all Canadians rather than just settling people's private debts for them.

There are other courts with special functions, and they are listed here only briefly.

Family Courts – provincial courts to handle domestic problems such as deserted wives.

Surrogate Courts – probate Wills and administer estates of persons who died with no Will.

Court of Revision – a special court where a taxpayer may dispute his property assessment for local taxes.

Juvenile Courts – now considered part of family court, to handle complaints against persons under the age of sixteen in Ontario.

The Art of Complaining

Legal action can be very costly. It might be just as effective to invest eight cents in a letter of complaint. Whether your problem is sales, service, guarantees, or unsafe products, some general rules apply about the art of complaining.

SOME GENERAL RULES

1. Be truthful. Don't alter the facts one bit. If the person investigating the complaint finds some falsehoods within, he may discharge the entire matter as false. Also, false accusations may result in a libel suit.

2. Be polite. A lot of name-calling and threats make a poor complaint. Just state what you are dissatisfied with and the remedy you would like.

3. Provide all the information. To save time, be sure to give the name, model number, serial number, year of manufacture, etc., of the product. Give the name of the store and date purchased. Make it exactly clear to the person reading your letter what has taken place and what must be done. Don't force him to write you a letter asking for more details.

COMPLAINING AT THE LOCAL LEVEL

1. Start with the source. Return to the seller, voice your complaint, and inquire what he proposes to do. Give the seller a fair chance to make good on his product before trying to make it difficult for him with someone else. If the salesman isn't cooperative, ask to speak with the owner or manager. Carefully file all sales slips and guarantees that came with the product.

2. Make a complaint to the local Chamber of Commerce or Better Business Bureau. Again, allow them reasonable time to act.

COMPLAINING AT A NATIONAL LEVEL

1. Write to the manufacturer of the product. If the only address shown is a city, you can obtain the street address from the long-distance telephone operator. Again, give full details in the letter of the complaint and of the action you have taken so far.

2. If the product is sold through a large chain store, write to the home office. Stores such as Eaton's list a customer service manager in their catalogue. Tell them why the local store did not provide satisfactory service.

3. If the complaint deals with a service instead of a product, see if there isn't an association which should be concerned. For example, insurance companies, stock brokers, mutual funds, the legal, medical, and accountancy professions all have associations that investigate complaints against their members.

COMPLAINING TO THE GOVERNMENT

There are far too many government agencies to list every single office. Here are some of the government agencies and departments which can act upon a complaint.

GOT A COMPLAINT?

Subject	Office
Consumer protection, credit, used cars, collection agencies, interest on loans, real estate brokers.	Consumer Protection Division Department of Financial and Commercial Affairs 555 Yonge Street Toronto 284, Ontario
Defective or dangerous product, false labelling or packaging.	Department of Consumer and Corporate Affairs Canadian Building 219 Laurier Avenue Ottawa 4, Ontario

False advertising, bait and switch advertising, false pricing.	Director, Combines Investigation Branch Department of Consumer and Corporate Affairs Ottawa, Ontario
Employment, wages or work conditions, job discrimination.	Ontario Department of Labour 74 Victoria Street Toronto, Ontario
Defective food or drugs.	Food and Drug Directorate Department of National Health and Welfare Tunney's Pasture Ottawa 3, Ontario
Insurance	Superintendent of Insurance 555 Yonge Street Toronto, Ontario

There is no guarantee that any government agency will agree with you or take action on your complaint.

Some Legal Jams

In this section, we examine some legal jams which citizens ordinarily get into. Let us assume that we are listening in while law students hear the tales that people bring to them everyday. The nature of this section will be conversation only; no detailed account of the legal procedures will be given. It is important that the reader not rely upon these cases to solve his own jams. Laws may have changed or the facts may be slightly, but significantly, different. Anyone with a legal jam should seek competent legal assistance.

The cases which follow should present to the reader some possible ideas as to how varied legal problems can be. Read them first for content, then review the material to pinpoint the legal principles involved, and try to determine how the legal jam might be averted, in this case and in similar cases in the future.

Case One

Mr. R. Adams, a machinist, brought with him a copy of a contract he had signed to purchase a new car.

Counsellor: "What's the problem with the car, Mr. Adams?"

Adams: "Delivery. I ordered a new car eleven weeks ago, and it took that long just to get it here. When it arrived, it wasn't what I ordered."

Counsellor: "How was it wrong?"

Adams: "The wrong colour and it had extra options I didn't order, like air-conditioning. I refused to accept it because it was $275 more expensive with those options. Am I right that I can refuse the car if it isn't what I ordered?"

Counsellor: "Yes. What's being done now?"

Adams: "The dealers re-ordered the car, but I'm not waiting another three months. My old car is a wreck, and I want to cancel the whole deal and buy a car right out of the showroom somewhere else. Can I get out of the deal?"

Counsellor: "Let me see the contract. (*pause*) Hmmm, it's a standard form. According to the terms on the back, you cannot break the contract."

Adams: "On the back? I never read anything on the back."

Counsellor: "Mr. Adams, on the front, just above the place where you signed, it says, "I have read and understand the terms on the back hereof and agree to them as part of this order as if they were printed above my signature."

Adams: "Oh, that. Well, I was in a hurry and the dealer should have told me what it said on the back. They can't hold me to something that I didn't read – that's crooked."

Counsellor: "Not at all. Now, let me read some of the terms aloud to you.

(3) I will accept delivery at the Vendor's premises of the Motor Vehicle and the optional equipment and accessories, if any, ordered herein (all of which are hereinafter called the Goods) within forty-eight hours after I have been notified that they are ready for delivery. Failure on my part to so accept delivery forfeits my cash deposit as liquidated damages for the Vendor's expense and efforts and permits him otherwise to dispose of the goods without any liability to me whatsoever.

Now, Mr. Adams, you made a down payment of $200. When the new car arrives, you will lose that if you don't accept it, providing it is the correct colour and with the correct options this time.

(4) Upon delivery of the Goods, time shall be of the essence in this order and agreement. If I default in making any payment due here-under or if I commit any breach of any of the terms hereof, or in the event of my bankruptcy, the whole balance of purchase price shall forthwith without demand become due and payable, and the Vendor or the Vendor's assigns may immediately repossess the goods and all attachments and may break and force open any enclosures and fasten-ings of any kind to secure access to the goods, and may remove, store, and repair same, and may sell same by public sale or by private sale or otherwise with or without notice and with or without advertising and upon such terms and for such price as the Vendor may deem best, and the net proceeds of such re-sale actually received after deducting all expenses of and incidental to repossession, storage, repair and sale, shall be applied on the sums payable hereunder, and the Vendor or the Vendor's assigns may enter suit for the deficiency for which I hereby agree to be liable. The rights of the Vendor are declared to be cumulative and not alternative and waiver of any default shall not constitute waiver of any other or subsequent default.

That's a long paragraph, and parts of it are not true. The Conditional Sales Act would require the dealer to hold the car twenty days before reselling it. He would have to inform you of the time and of the place where it would be sold. What is important to you is that when the car arrives and you don't accept it, you are in breach of contract and the entire amount of the car becomes due immediately. Failure to pay would jeopardize you more in that the dealer could sell it for less to someone else and require you to repay him the difference.

(7) The Vendor shall not be liable for any delay or failure to make delivery for any cause whatsoever, and this order and agreement shall not be binding upon the Vendor until accepted by him or by one of his employees who is duly authorized in writing.

Legally, the delays or mistakes in getting you the right car cannot be used as an excuse to break the contract. There is no time limit mentioned in the contract at all for the dealer to get you the right car. I don't know the dealer in question, but I suspect a certain dishonesty in the matter."

Adams: "What sort of dishonesty?"

Counsellor: "It is conceivable that he deliberately ordered a car with added options. After a long wait, he hoped you would accept the extras and pay the added $275 because of your impatience to get the car. His profit on extras is very high."

Adams: "How can I prove it?"

Counsellor: "It's very near impossible. Also, it might have been a legitimate mistake."

Adams: "So there's nothing I can do but wait?"

Counsellor: "Not exactly nothing. Here's my advice:

1. Discuss the matter with the dealer and ask him to tear up the contract. If he agrees, make sure you see him do it. He might promise to do it, then change his mind, and you are still hooked.

2. If the dealer refuses, check the local Chamber of Commerce. Ask about previous complaints against the dealer and file a complaint of your own.

3. Make a photocopy of this order form. Send it to the manufacturer and ask for a check of their records to see if what you ordered and what the dealer ordered from the factory are the same thing. Find out where the mistake was made.

4. File a complaint with the Department of Financial and Commercial Affairs, 555 Yonge Street, Toronto 284, Ontario."

Adams: "What will this achieve?"

Counsellor: "Perhaps nothing. This is called the 'heat' treatment. These agencies will all request an explanation or investigation. The dealer may decide it's better to get you off his back by tearing up the contract."

Adams: "If it doesn't work, then what?"

Counsellor: "Read the contract before you sign – next time."

Case Two

Mrs. R. Thorn, housewife, brought with her a Conditional Sales Contract she had signed. The contract was for the purchase of a vacuum cleaner. She had signed it after a demonstration by a door-to-door salesman.

Counsellor: "What is your legal question?"

Thorn: "I've simply got to get this contract cancelled. My husband travels, and he wasn't home when the machine was demonstrated. It was a very impressive demonstration, and the machine cleaned far better than my present one. But, when my husband got home, he was furious."

Counsellor: "Over the price?"

Thorn: "Exactly. He hit the ceiling when he saw the terms."

Counsellor: "May I see the contract? (*pause*) You agreed to pay 12 monthly installments of $21 each, or a total of $252 for the machine. This figure is broken down as $225 for the machine and $27 interest. That's a very high price for a vacuum cleaner. I'd say you could buy the same machine in a store for $130 at the most."

Thorn: "That's what my husband said."

Counsellor: "Why did you agree to pay so much?"

Thorn: "Well, the salesman said that I would not have to pay that much in the long run. He asked for the names of fifty of my friends. He told me that for every machine he sold to one of them, he would rebate twenty-five dollars to me. If he sold a machine to just six or eight of the fifty, I'd get the machine for almost nothing. He was a very good salesman, and the machine was just marvellous. It cleans like nothing I've ever seen."

Counsellor: "The sales technique is called referral selling, and at the moment it is quite legal. In the near future, if the Competition Act is passed, it will be illegal."

Thorn: "What's wrong with it?"

Counsellor: "The name gimmick. It is doubtful that he will sell a machine to any of your friends, especially when they see that price. You're not going to get any rebates, and you are going to pay $252 for that machine"

Thorn: "Can I get out of it? My husband says he won't pay for it, and I don't know how I'm going to find the money. One of my friends told me that I can't sign contracts unless my husband signs too. Is that right?"

Counsellor: "No, it isn't. A married woman in Ontario has the legal power to sign contracts in her name, without her husband's consent or knowledge for that matter. Many women do not allow their husbands to know their business matters. You can sue or be sued, and your husband has nothing to do with it."

Thorn: "Well, isn't there something in the law that says you can't sign contracts in your home?"

Counsellor: "No. The provision I believe you are thinking about is in the Consumer Protection Act and it gives a two-day cooling off period for contracts signed in a home. You had two days to change your mind and notify this company. Unfortunately, more than ten days have passed."

Thorn: "If they sue me, does my husband have to pay?"

Counsellor: "Not at all. You must be held liable on the contract. If you have any assets at all, such as a bank account, you will find that the court will garnishee those assets to enforce payment."

Thorn: "You mean a judge would side with them and make someone pay twice what something is worth? Won't they at least lower the price for me?"

Counsellor: "The court does not make personal bargains for people. Unless the interest rate is excessive, which it is not, the court cannot assume to know what value people place on things. What you think is a bad bargain another person might rate as a fair bargain."

Thorn: "Is there no possible way out?"

Counsellor: "It would appear there is not. I would recommend that you send a letter to the Consumer Protection Division, Department of Financial and Commercial Affairs, 555

55

Yonge Street, Toronto 284, Ontario. It is doubtful whether they can do much for you, but they are interested in documenting cases like yours. Also, if the salesman did not hold a licence as a transient trader, you might be able to avoid the contract, but he probably has a licence. Also, advise the Chamber of Commerce that this trader is in town as a warning to others to be wary. Your bad experience can serve as a lesson to others. In the future, discuss things with your husband before signing contracts or making purchases."

Thorn: "I usually do, but the salesman said I had to sign right then or the special offer lapsed."

Counsellor: "That's an old sales trick to try and stampede the customers into signing right away before they think it over and realize what a poor bargain they are getting. This is one of the reasons the two-day cooling off period was brought into our law. Unfortunately, the lesson has been an expensive one for you."

Case Three

Thomas Burnett, age 19, came into the office using a cane. He explained that he had just been released from the hospital.

Counsellor: "Where does your legal problem lie, with the accident?"

Burnett: "Not exactly, It's my car. The finance company repossessed it because I didn't keep up the payments. I had an operation on my knee and haven't worked for four months. I couldn't keep up the payments on the car. I only had it a year. My Dad tried to help, but he couldn't keep up either, they were pretty expensive payments."

Counsellor: "What were the original terms of the agreement?"

Burnett: "Well, the car was to cost $3,400.00. I made a down payment of $500.00 and agreed to finance the remaining $2,700.00. I was paying $109.50 a month for 30 months. That comes to $3,285.00 – or $585.00 interest."

Counsellor: "I'm with you so far."

Burnett: "Okay, so I missed two payments and the finance company came and repossessed my car. Then, they sent me a statement showing everything I still owed, but they added on stuff like cost of repossessing, storage, and insurance. Can they do that?"

Counsellor: "Yes, provided the amounts they charge for repossessing, storage, and insurance are reasonable."

Burnett: "They also said that if I don't pay the full amount within twenty days, they will sell the car as second hand and if they don't get enough money to pay my bill I will still owe them the difference. Can they do that?"

Counsellor: "Absolutely. The only provision is that they must sell the car to a third party for a fair market price. They cannot buy the car themselves nor can they sacrifice the car for some absurd fee such as one dollar. However, if the sale doesn't bring in enough to cover what you owe, you still owe the difference. If the sale brings in more than you owe, they must refund the difference to you. However, that seldom happens since the car is second hand. You will probably end up still owing them several hundred dollars."

Burnett: "How can it be that I paid $500 down and made the payments for almost a year, and then I lose the car and still owe them money?"

Counsellor: "You received the use of the car for a year, and you caused the car to depreciate rapidly. Depreciation is fastest during the first year. The car they repossessed isn't new at all any more, they will end up selling it for about half of what you paid for it."

Burnett: "What can I do to avoid this?"

Counsellor: "Well, you can discuss the matter with the finance company manager. If you have prospects of going back to work soon, perhaps he is willing to extend credit to you a little longer. If not, you may be able to borrow the money from another source. Usually this is a terribly costly business and I wouldn't recommend it to most people, but you have a particularly difficult problem. You will be borrowing money and paying interest in order to pay off another debt upon which you owe interest. That is poor policy, but it may be your only solution. You may not be able to get credit elsewhere unless you can provide collateral. If you cannot raise the entire balance owed, I'm afraid your car will be sold and you will still owe quite a bit of money."

Burnett: "Well, I'll try talking to the finance company first."

Counsellor: "It's certainly worth a try. They aren't in the car business and don't really want to repossess and sell cars. If you can convince them at all of your ability to get back to work and make up back payments, I think they will give you another opportunity. One precaution – don't refinance it with them. That will be deadly expensive, worse than letting them sell it. In the future, I suggest you save your money before you buy rather than finance for such a long term. When you bought the car, $109.50 a month didn't seem like a lot. But, if you got married or lost your job, paying $109.50 a month for 30 months for a car can suddenly become a terrific burden. You might have settled for a used car rather than a new one. Keep that in mind in future deals."

Case Four

Roger Stoll, age 35, an accountant, presented a new problem. He was seeking legal advice about a problem he had with a lawyer.

Counsellor:	"Give me the details."
Stoll:	"Well, I bought a parcel of land to build on, and had a lawyer handle all the matters. I was always told to have a lawyer handle vital financial matters like that. Also, I got a mortgage company to put up most of the money and they insisted that a lawyer be involved."
Counsellor:	"That has traditionally been sound advice."
Stoll:	"Well, this time it wasn't. The lawyer had all the work done by a young lawyer who was just an apprentice and he made a mistake. A big one."
Counsellor:	"There's no such thing as an apprentice lawyer, really. What you mean is an articling student-at-law."
Stoll:	"Whatever he was doing, it was wrong. I ended up short about one-fourth my land."
Counsellor:	"How?"
Stoll:	"Why, the Offer to Buy that I signed stated that the lot was 200 feet deep and 160 feet wide. The Deed I got says the lot is 200 feet deep and 120 feet wide. My lawyer approved the whole transaction and I concluded the sale on his advice."
Counsellor:	"What you are saying is the Offer to Buy was incorrectly drawn and when the articling student checked the title he did not notice this discrepancy?"
Stoll:	"That's right. I thought I was getting a lot 160 feet wide and got only 120 feet. I found out when I put a fence up and my neighbour told me I was putting it on his land. I got the Deed and found out he was right. Now, my question is what can I do?"
Counsellor:	"Who made out the Offer to Buy?"

Stoll:	"The real estate agent."
Counsellor:	"Well, the sale is final, I don't think you can do anything about that. The real estate agent was negligent, and you should file a complaint with the Ontario Department of Financial and Commercial Affairs, The Registrar of Real Estate, 555 Yonge Street, Toronto 284, Ontario. All real estate brokers are licensed and this government office will look into the question of why the Offer to Buy was drawn up incorrectly. Now, have you made inquiries to the lawyer about this?"
Stoll:	"Yes, and he acknowledged that there was a mistake but said there was nothing to be done."
Counsellor:	"I'm surprised, because lawyers have insurance policies that protect them if they err and are sued later. That's just about what you will have to/do."
Stoll:	"Is he liable? He acts like there's nothing I can do."
Counsellor:	"Did you pay him for the work?"
Stoll:	"Yes, $300. Does that make a difference?"
Counsellor:	"Sometimes. If he gave you free advice, he may not be liable. If he accepted your fee as a client, he is duty bound to be diligent and make no mistakes. Lawyers, like bankers and accountants, have a special duty of care in the work they do for their clients. Your financial loss is due to his mistake and is his legal responsibility. You will have to hire another lawyer and sue the first lawyer."
Stoll:	"Sounds like a vicious circle."
Counsellor:	"It's unusual that you would have to take such drastic steps. Most lawyers are eager to insure their clients are well looked after. However, these difficulties can arise. You must first have the value of the land you lost estimated for you so that you will know the amount you are suing for. After that, your lawyer will do the rest."

Case Five

Mr. and Mrs. Eldon Johnson came into the office to discuss a problem they were having with medical bills.

Counsellor:	"What did the bills arise from?"
Mr. Johnson:	"From an automobile accident. Our son David was riding with another boy in the car. The car belongs to the father of the other boy. He's 17, David is 16. They were out Friday night in the car. It left the road and hit a tree and both boys were badly injured. This was two months ago. David is home now, but the bills from the accident have been terrible for us to pay. A friend told us we should sue the father of the boy who was driving. He owns the car, and our friend said if we sue, his insurance company would pay everything. What do you think?"
Counsellor:	"Off hand, I'd say you are wrong."
Mrs. Johnson:	"Why? The police say the car must have been going at least 70 judging by the damages. There was beer in the car, too."
Counsellor:	"In some provinces, I might give you a different answer, but in Ontario, I think you have little chance of collecting. In some instances, the insurance company may offer some sums just to insure that you don't sue later. However, I believe they are under no liability here at all, since your son was a passenger in the car, not in another car struck by this car. Now, the Ontario Highway Traffic Act states that, 'the owner or driver of a motor vehicle other than a vehicle operated in the business of carrying passengers for compensation shall not be liable for any loss or damage resulting from bodily injury to, or the death of any person being carried in, or upon, or

getting on to, or alighting from the motor vehicle, except where such loss or damage was caused or contributed to by the gross negligence of the driver of the motor vehicle.' "

Mr. Johnson: "Can you explain that in simpler words?"

Counsellor: "It means that passengers who are riding with another person cannot hold him responsible unless he was guilty of gross negligence. This does not include persons who are paying for their ride, such as those aboard buses or taxis. Your case would be one where David was a gratuitous passenger riding with the other boy. The law says the driver or owner are not responsible for his injury, unless it can be shown the driver was guilty of gross negligence in his driving."

Mr. Johnson: "What is gross negligence?"

Counsellor: "A very hard thing to define. One judge simply called it a very great negligence and let it go at that. There are many terms in our statutes which are difficult to define. Many cases have been fought over what gross negligence means. Roughly, I would tell you that negligence is omitting to do something which a reasonable man would do, or doing something which a prudent and reasonable man would not do. Negligence is failure to take care not to injure your neighbour where you could foresee that you might injure him. Gross, while having many meanings, in this sense would mean very great."

Mr. Johnson: "Why don't you think this was gross negligence on the part of the driver?"

Counsellor: "The main problem is proof. The fact that the car left the road and hit the tree is not proof in itself of gross negligence. There must be more substantial proof that the driver was driving in a very negligent manner."

Mrs. Johnson: "What about the presence of beer in the car? The police said they found beer bottles scattered about, and broken bottles in the car."

Counsellor: "It is contrary to the Ontario Liquor Control Act to have opened bottles in the car, but there is no proof here of there having been drinking in the car. Nor does this matter; it does not prove the driver was driving negligently. Another point – in Ontario it is generally assumed that a person who rides with another on a free basis accepts the risks involved. That is, he voluntarily subjects himself to the danger. The law assumes that the passenger knows whether or not the driver is a safe driver, or can quickly figure that out. If he continues to ride with him, despite the fact that he knows he is reckless or speeds, then he cannot later complain if he is injured. In Latin, it is expressed, *Volenti non fit injuria,* or 'That to which a man consents cannot be considered an injury'. I think this fits your case somewhat."

Mr. Johnson: "Well, you don't think we can successfully sue?"

Counsellor: "No, I don't. You can always try, but I think your chances of success are small since there is no evidence of gross negligence at this point. I would suggest contacting the insurance company and inquiring if they wish to make any settlement at all under the medical coverages of the policy. As far as a major law suit is concerned, I would urge you to forget it."

Case Six

Jerry Dewald, age 19, came into the office looking very successful for a person of his few years.

Counsellor: "You look like someone who has just scored, rather than someone with a problem."

Dewald: "I don't think I have a problem. I just want you to read a contract for me before I sign it. Just to make sure there aren't any sneaky parts."

Counsellor: "What sort of contract?"

Dewald: "Well, I just finished a special course on cosmetics. It was really a fabulous course and now I'm going to have my own franchise. I'll be the main distributor in this area and hire other people to canvass for me."

Counsellor: "Why are you so sure it will be successful?"

Dewald: "We had this dinner at the end of the course and the company had some other franchise dealers come in and talk to us. They're really cleaning up. Some are making $20,000 a year."

Counsellor: "Did you see any proof of that?"

Dewald: "No, but they seemed honest enough. Besides, why would they lie?"

Counsellor: "Maybe because they were paid to. Maybe they aren't dealers at all, just hired actors. May I see the contract?" *(pause)*

Counsellor: "You have not entered into any agreement as yet, is that right?"

Dewald: "Not yet."

Counsellor: "My advice is to forget this."

Dewald: "Why? It can't miss."

Counsellor: "For the company it can't miss. For you it can go very much amiss. You would agree to buy outright from the company a first installment of $5,000 worth of cos-

65

	metics. For this you would sign a promissory note. Then, over the next three years, you agree to purchase $10,000 more in cosmetics."
Dewald:	"Yeah – I know that. I can buy more at a reduced price if I want."
Counsellor:	"Now, let's be realistic. Do you think that anyone, or any team or group of persons could sell $15,000 worth of cosmetics door-to-door in the next three years?"
Dewald:	"Certainly, It's a top line, and last year Canadians spent over $1 billion on cosmetics and other beauty aids."
Counsellor:	"That may be the case, but your prices would be much higher than retail stores. There are other, established firms going door-to-door. You know what I think will happen?"
Dewald:	"What?"
Counsellor:	"You will sell about one-third of this if you are lucky and be liable to buy the remainder, which will sit in your apartment or basement. This is called pyramid selling and in the near future I believe it will be illegal. The company dumps huge amounts on you, and you must find other persons to sell for you so you can dump it on them."
Dewald:	"I still think it can be done. Some of those dealers were selling two or three times that amount."
Counsellor:	"So they told you. Remember what I said – they may have been just hired to impress you with big talk. Once you sign this, you will be committed to something you may regret. If sales interest you, get into a legitimate sales position. Stay clear of pyramid selling like this."
Dewald:	"Well, I'll keep what you said in mind."
Counsellor:	"I hope so. Somehow I suspect that I didn't convince you. If you want some more advice, check with the local Chamber of Commerce. They'll tell you much the same. Whatever you decide, investigate fully before you sign."

Case Seven

Mrs. Elizabeth Small, retired, entered the office looking somewhat apprehensive.

Counsellor: "You seem ill at ease, Mrs. Small. Have we upset you in some way?"

Small: "No, I just expected a more formal office."

Counsellor: "I must apologize. Our funds are limited, but we think our service is still the best. How can we help you?"

Small: "I want to buy some property. A friend suggested that I would be hasty to buy before making some inquiries."

Counsellor: "Where is the property?"

Small: "It's in Florida. It's a new development called West Wind City. I have a brochure here. You see, I'm retired and want to live more modestly. Also, I find the winters here rather severe and Florida sounds so much nicer. Some of my friends have already moved there."

Counsellor: "May I see the brochure?"
(pause)

Counsellor: "These illustrations are just drawings, Mrs. Small. None of this has been constructed yet at all."

Small: "Oh I know that. They explained all that in the book. But you see, a small house, on one level, will cost only $9,000. They're just beautiful. And there's going to be a shaded drive, a shopping centre, schools, everything."

Counsellor: "You think all those things will exist, but at the moment none of them do and there is no guarantee they will be built. Where is this West Wind City?"

Small: "It's shown on the map."

Counsellor: "Yes, I see a big star on the map, and that would not be very useful when driving in a car. How does one get there, exactly?"

Small: "I don't really know. I haven't been there."

Counsellor:	"Well, here is my advice. You say you have friends in Florida. Write to them and ask them to try and find this West Wind City and report back to you. That's the first step. Then, write to the Chamber of Commerce in the nearest large city, which seems to be Tampa, and ask them if they ever heard of it. Don't sign anything until you get reports back."
Small:	"Do you think there is something wrong with it?"
Counsellor:	"Mrs. Small, people have bought more swampland in Florida than there are lakes in Ontario. These brochures abound, and many of them are false. It is unlawful to advertise the sale of foreign real estate in Ontario without a licence. How did you get this?"
Small:	"By mail."
Counsellor:	"That should raise some suspicion in your mind."
Small:	"Yes, it did, but once I read the descriptions . . ."
Counsellor:	"Descriptions of things that don't exist, Mrs. Small. Remember that. I would wait until your friends have contacted you, and best of all – go there yourself before you decide."
Small:	"Thank you, I will. You may have prevented me from making a bad mistake."
Counsellor:	"I hope that it turns out to be legitimate, for your sake. But I sincerely doubt it."

Case Eight

Mr. T. Cochrane, somewhat elderly, entered the office with a predetermined look of "I bet you can't help me."

Counsellor:	"What can I do to be of service."
Cochrane:	"You tell me how to get rid of them bums!"
Counsellor:	"Sir?"
Cochrane:	"Them squatters in my house."
Counsellor:	"Can you expand that a bit?"
Cochrane:	"I rented a house to a couple. They looked O.K., and had just one kid. I rented it to them for $150 a month. Only has two bedrooms. They looked clean."
Counsellor:	"Something has gone wrong with the tenancy?"
Cochrane:	"Must be twenty of them living in there now. Just a bunch of squatters. I shoulda known."
Counsellor:	"He had more than two children?"
Cochrane:	"Not him. First it was her mother. Said she was old and sickly. No one to look after her. Then it was his sister, said she needed help looking after the mother. Then, the sister turns up pregnant, marries the stiff, and has the baby. They're all living in there, in two bedrooms. That's eight people. I told 'em that's too many, but they said there's no law about that as long as they're clean. Is that right?"
Counsellor:	"The Department of Health can't act unless there is a health problem. Did you have them sign a lease?"
Cochrane:	"Yeah, here it is. Bought it in a store."
Counsellor:	"I see. There's nothing in this lease about the number of persons living in the house. You could have limited that if you wanted."
Cochrane:	"I suppose, but like I said, they looked like good people. Now they're all in there like squatters and I can't get them out, can I?"

Counsellor:	"Not under this lease. I can only advise you how to get them out eventually. When the lease runs out, and it is for one year, send them written notification that the rent will be $400 a month. I suspect they will move rather than pay that amount."
Cochrane:	"That'll do it, eh?"
Counsellor:	"Yes. It's a one-year lease, so you must give them the notice at least sixty days before the lease runs out. It's a tough way to deal with tenants, but sometimes it has to be done. Not all tenants play fair with their landlords."
Cochrane:	"How do I prevent it from happening again?"
Counsellor:	"In the lease, include this phrase, 'The lessee covenants with the lessor that the premises shall be occupied only by the lessee and his immediate family, to include his wife and children. The lessee further covenants with the lessor not to permit other members of his family, visitors, guests, servants, or persons transacting business to reside within or upon the premises without the consent in writing of the lessor.' "
Cochrane:	"That'll do it?"
Counsellor:	"I believe so. Sorry we couldn't do anything for you at the present."
Cochrane:	"That's O.K. I really didn't expect you could."

Case Nine

E. Walton, a fairly elderly man obviously dressed in working clothes, entered the office.

Counsellor: "Mr. Walton, have a seat."

Walton: "I won't waste your time. I'm mad as hell about my insurance company."

Counsellor: "Auto insurance?"

Walton: "No, property insurance. I had this insurance properly made out and all and paid premiums for years and now they won't pay me when I have a claim. I run a small business, just a general store and small machinery shop – lawn mowers in the summer and snow blowers in the winter. I insured my building and stock. Last week a snow blower was stolen from outside the building. Not all my stock is inside, there ain't room and I demonstrate them outside. Now, I specifically told my agent that some of my stock sits outside and he said that was O.K. and everything was covered. Somebody stole a $400 snow blower and the company refuses to pay. They said a thing left outside like that is left at my risk. Too easy to steal they said."

Counsellor: "Did you inform them that the agent told you it would be protected?"

Walton: "Yes, but they said he was wrong and that what he says ain't important, it's what the policy says."

Counsellor: "May I see the policy?"

Walton: "I don't have it. I got so mad, I went down there and just threw the thing at them and said if that's the way they feel about it just cancel the thing. After paying all those premiums and all."

Counsellor: "You returned the policy and cancelled it."

Walton: "That I did."

71

Counsellor:	"That makes it very difficult to advise you what the policy said, since you don't have it any more."
Walton:	"I guess so, but nobody can read those things anyway. Don't make one bit of sense."
Counsellor:	"I agree partly with you, there. Well, not having the policy to examine, it will be very much guesswork as to what we can do now. Here's what I recommend to you: 1. Write a letter to the insurance company. Advise them that you believe that under the policy which you held your machine was insured. Remind them of the agent's statement that the policy he sold you provided full coverage indoors or outside. Send the letter registered mail. Demand an accounting that they pay the claim or state the reason why they will not. 2. If you don't get a reply within three weeks, or if you receive a reply explaining why they do not feel you are covered, send a letter stating your case to the Superintendent of Insurance, 555 Yonge Street, Toronto, Ontario. Ask for an investigation by the Superintendent's office."
Walton:	"You think that will work?"
Counsellor:	"Mr. Walton, it is very difficult to say because I really don't know what the policy says. Without the policy, we are proceeding very blindly. There is one important factor in your favour and that is what the agent told you. Granted, he might deny ever telling you that your stock was insured outside and your case will probably die right there. Without proof and without a policy, it is unlikely you will succeed. If the agent admits he told you that your stock was insured outside, then prospects are brighter. The Superintendent may order either the company or the agent to make good the claim on the grounds that the policy you bought was misrepresented to you regarding what it provided. If nothing else, you still retain the right to sue the agent for misrepresentation, provided he admits making such a statement to you."
Walton:	"Well, it don't look too bright to me. I might as well forget it."

72

Counsellor: "Don't surrender yet. At least do the two things I advised you to do, and come back and let me know the outcome. We can discuss any further action then."

Walton: "All right, I'll do that much. I suppose I can invest in a couple of postage stamps for a $400 machine I lost."

Counsellor: "If anything like that happens in the future, don't cancel or return the policy until the claim matter has been settled. You surrendered your best piece of evidence."

Case Ten

W. Sampson was convinced he was right when he explained his problem with a credit card.

Counsellor: "A bill you don't owe, Mr. Sampson?"

Sampson: "Sort of. I lost my gasoline credit card. Actually, I lost my whole wallet and it was in there. Now, I sent a letter to the gasoline company and told them the card was lost. They acknowledged my letter. Everything seemed fine."

Counsellor: "Now it isn't?"

Sampson: "No. The person who found my wallet went on a spree! He's rented a car and disappeared with it. The rental company is after me for the value of a brand new car!"

Counsellor: "That could be expensive. How many days later did the finder rent the car?"

Sampson: "The next day. I got a call from the car rental company asking where the car was. I said what car? They said I rented a car for two days and three weeks later the car was still not returned. Anyway, they said a man walked in with a credit card and driver's licence, etc., all in my name. That's simple because I lost the entire wallet. He's stolen the car, and they're after me for it. Can they collect from me?"

Counsellor: "A difficult matter Mr. Sampson. There are certain items which you would definitely be responsible for. For example, if the thief ran up a hotel bill, meals, gasoline, and other items on your credit card in the short period of time which it takes the credit card company to notify all its subscribers that your card has been stolen, you would have to pay for all those things. This is one of the risks of having a card that gets into another person's hands, particularly when all your identification also gets into their hands at the same time. A merchant who asks for proof of identity before honouring a card would accept the other things in the wallet as proof. This is a growing racket. Cards are stolen by the thousand and turned into profits by buying such things as expensive airlines tickets then turning the tickets back in for a cash refund. Other thieves simply go on a spending spree at your expense. However, as to a car that was stolen, it is a difficult matter. I can't say I ever heard about a similar case."

Sampson: "Must I pay for the value of the car?"

Counsellor: "At first glance, I would say that you do not have to buy the car outright from them."

Sampson: "That's a relief."

Counsellor: "*But* . . . . let's not forget that the car was rented, and legally it was rented by you, although someone impersonated you. They can continue to charge you rent until the vehicle is found."

Sampson: "What if it is never found?"

Counsellor: "Then I would guess that the rent could run upwards until it finally reached the full value of the car. Perhaps it might go even higher, although I think the court would be inclined to cut it off when the full value of the car was paid."

Sampson: "Good grief."

Counsellor: "Mind you, I can't recall a similar case, although one may exist. At the moment, I can only suggest two things to you:

1. Notify the rental company that the person who used your card was not entitled to use it. Make no statement that you accept responsibility for anything.

2. Request from the rental company a full description of the missing car and advise police yourself that it is stolen. The rental company may already have done so, but just make sure by doing it yourself."

Sampson: "What if they sue me?"

Counsellor: "Then, sir, you must hire a lawyer and be prepared to argue the claim in court. The chief problem is that the thief got the car before your notification reached the gasoline credit card company. Another day or so would have made all the difference. It would have been worth it to telephone them long distance rather than write a letter. The telephone call would have been faster. Remember that next time."

Sampson: "There won't be a next time. I'll never own another one of the !*(± @ #$ things."

Counsellor: "They have advantages – and they do have their risks."

Case Eleven

Mr. and Mrs. R. Pauley came prepared to discuss a question that many people have raised and had identical troubles with – their lease.

Counsellor: "I understand you rent your house?"

Mr. Pauley: "Yes, from a retired gentleman who owns several houses which he rents for his living. Recently, he sold the house and the new owner has demanded we move out."

Counsellor: "Have you a written lease with the previous landlord?"

Mr. Pauley: "Yes, I brought it along. It's a yearly lease, and it doesn't terminate for another eight months. The new owner wants to live in the house and he isn't interested in leasing it to us, he wants us out."

Counsellor: "How did he serve eviction upon you?"

Mrs. Pauley: "He brought a written eviction order and gave it to me personally."

Counsellor: "Who signed the lease?"

Mr. Pauley: "I did."

Counsellor: "Well, then the eviction order was not served correctly on you and you could ignore it anyway. The Landlord and Tenant Act requires that the landlord serve the order personally upon the tenant. Mr. Pauley is the tenant, not Mrs. Pauley. Now, if Mr. Pauley were avoiding the landlord or was absent for a prolonged period, it would be acceptable to serve the notice on Mrs. Pauley, who is an adult residing with the tenant."

Mr. Pauley: "So the eviction order has no effect?"

Counsellor: "At the moment, no. But that's not the main point, anyway. Since your lease came into existence before the agreement of sale of the house, then you cannot be forced by the new owner to vacate until the lease runs out. Your lease must be respected by the new landlord just as it was binding on the previous landlord. Now, if the mortgage company was foreclosing on the property because the mortgage wasn't paid, and the mortgage was registered before the lease was signed, then the mortgage company could order you out. But, that does not seem to be the case here. Your lease, being a written one-year lease, cannot be pushed aside by a new landlord. He is now your new landlord and you should pay your rent to him."

Mrs. Pauley: "We tried, but he refused the rent. He said that because our lease wasn't registered we lost our rights."

Counsellor: "Not so. A lease may be registered and that will insure rights against practically all comers, but it is not necessary in this case to register the lease to enforce it. When the new owner was considering the property as a purchase, he must have known you were living in it. He must have realized that you have a tenancy agreement with the man who sold the house. It would be his obligation to find out the length of the lease, and when it would expire. Failing to do this, he will have to wait until your lease expires before ordering you out and moving in himself."

Mr. Pauley: "Are you sure? He said that we are overholding and will have to pay him double rent for every month we stay."

Counsellor: "You are not overholding. A tenant overholds who must lawfully give up a property and refuses to do so. Since he will not accept your offer to pay your rent, you should protect yourself further by paying the correct amount of rent into the court. This will demonstrate that you carried out the terms of your lease. Whenever he wants his rent, he can go to the court and collect it."

Mr. Pauley: "Well, that certainly reassures us. We really haven't a place to move to right now."

Counsellor: "You will eventually have to leave, but you have until the end of your lease period to find another place. Good luck, and if there are any further arguments with the new owner, feel free to contact me again. In the meantime, don't forget to pay your rent into the court each month so he can't claim you failed or refused to pay rent and evict you on that ground."

Case Twelve

Tim Irving, age 19, came into the office and sprawled confidently into a chair.

Counsellor: "A problem? You look quite confident."

Irving: "I am, really, but I thought I would make sure. I sold my car to this guy. He came around to my house and looked it over, and we agreed on a price of $600. It's in pretty good shape, although it isn't new or anything like that."

Counsellor: "Something went wrong with the sale?"

Irving: "He said he definitely wanted it, see. So, I said he should give me a down payment or something, so he gave me $20 and I gave him a receipt. He said he had to get the rest of the dough from the bank. He was supposed to come back the next day. He didn't come back for four days, and then he brought another guy with him."

Counsellor: "He must have had second thoughts."

Irving: "Right. He was talking to this great friend of his and this guy says that $600 is much too much for the car and that he should get it for about $450. He comes back and says he is only prepared to pay $450. His friend walks around and really talks like the car is a wreck and everything. So, I say a deal is a deal and it goes for $600. He backs out and wants the $20 back he made as a down payment. I said he wasn't getting the twenty, it's mine."

Counsellor: "I'm with you so far."

Irving: "Well, he's really mad and the other guy is telling him that he should be glad he didn't really get clipped, see. So, I told him I didn't have the $20 anyway, I spent it. I really didn't have it, cause I spent it all that night. He said he will be back this Saturday for the money. Do I owe him the $20?"

Counsellor:	"No, you are right that you may keep it. What you entered into was a contract of sale. Since the value of the car is more than $40, the contract really should have been in writing. However, by giving you a down payment and you giving him a receipt, the sale was made final, even without a written contract. He is the one who has violated the agreement and cannot insist that you return the down payment. The partial payment was a way of showing his good faith to carry out his end of the bargain. However, there is no actual proof that $600 was the price you two agreed to."
Irving:	"No, but he agreed to it all right. Actually, he isn't too swift a thinker, if you know what I mean. His buddy was a better car trader than him."
Counsellor:	"The fact that he made a bad bargain does not excuse him. His poor judgement in agreeing to pay $600 when the car is perhaps not worth that much is not a defence to later refuse to go through with the sale. Actually, it is you who can insist he pay the rest of the money and complete the sale. However, without any written proof that he agreed to pay $600 it would be better to forget that. However, the $20 remains yours until he carries out the rest of the contract. If he refuses, then it must be concluded that he forfeits the amount. You may regard it as compensation for holding the car for him and refusing to sell it to someone else. You see, if another person had come along after him and offered you $700, you would have to turn him down, saying the car was already sold."
Irving:	"Yeah, but nobody did."
Counsellor:	"It doesn't matter, the principle is the same. You may keep the $20 for your troubles, for his breach of contract, and for having given up any opportunity to sell the car to someone else."
Irving:	"Glad you said that. Isn't there any way he can get back at me?"
Counsellor:	"Not legally, but if he is a violent type, take care he doesn't try to extract the $20 in your flesh and blood."
Irving:	"I will. Man, I hope somebody else comes along and does the same thing. Those $20 deposits could add up."

Case Thirteen

Mr. C. Holtrop came into the office to discuss a property problem he had been having.

Counsellor: "What sort of problem?"

Holtrop: "Trespassers, sort of. Every winter I get more and more snowmobiles running over my property."

Counsellor: "Your yard?"

Holtrop: "No, it's just a field behind my place. It isn't good for much and I really don't object to folks driving over it. What worries me is that someone will get hurt. There's lots of bad holes in that field and when the snow is deep, you can't see them. I have a snowmobile myself, and I know pretty well where the bad spots are. What I'm worried about is someone really getting hurt and suing me."

Counsellor: "What you fear could just happen. Normally, a person who enters your property or crosses over it is trespassing, but if you give approval or consent, even silent or tacit approval, it could be said that you have given them licence to cross your property. Having given them licence, you would be responsible if they hit a hazard that you knew of and failed to warn them about."

Holtrop: "I hate to fence them out, some are friends of mine, and we all use each other's property somewhat."

Counsellor: "A difficult position, but I don't think you can try to straddle the fence. You cannot allow persons to have easy and continual access to your property and still try to say that you are not liable for any injuries. You must make up your mind whether you will call them trespassers or whether you are willing to allow them access, making them guests in a certain sense. If they are guests, then you must take the responsibility for their safety as regards dangers about which you know. You

81

	would have to go out and mark all the worst spots with markers of some kind, etc."
Holtrop:	"I really don't think I could mark them all . . . there's so many."
Counsellor:	"What you are saying, it seems, is that the field is not a safe place for snowmobiles."
Holtrop:	"No, it really isn't a good place for it."
Counsellor:	"Then, you leave yourself no choice but to deter others from driving there. Either fence it off, or as a minimum post a sign to the effect that it is dangerous and snow-mobiles are prohibited. This will make it clear that you do not give specific or tacit licence to drive in the field. Post the sign in a conspicuous place where drivers enter."
Holtrop:	"Can I explain to a few friends that the sign doesn't mean them, if they are careful about it?"
Counsellor:	"No. You cannot post a sign saying one thing and then tell persons the opposite. You may apologize, but re-member it is for their own safety that you must exclude drivers. If they still ignore the sign, then they do so at their own risk, but you must never indicate that you will tolerate those who ignore your warning. At all times, your official attitude must be that you do not per-mit snowmobiles."
Holtrop:	"My friends are sure gonna be sore."
Counsellor:	"Your friends would often be quick to sue you."
Holtrop:	"Maybe I'll just try to get an insurance policy on the property to protect me."
Counsellor:	"That's another method, but it sidesteps rather than solves the problem."
Holtrop:	"Well, thanks anyway, but I guess I'll just take a chance that no one gets hurt."
Counsellor:	"That's a chance I wouldn't want to bet on. But, good luck to you anyway."

Case Fourteen

Mrs. D. Laverty entered the office to discuss a question regarding a deceased person's estate.

Counsellor: "A problem with the Will?"

Laverty: "Yes, in a way. A very old friend passed away, and her estate is being settled and property disposed of. She had no living relatives, and few friends, except for myself and another neighbour. For many years, she promised me a beautiful cabinet she owned. It's a huge thing, mostly hand worked, with a glass front, quite expensive. But the value isn't important. It was something personal that she wanted me to have."

Counsellor: "I'm afraid to ask the next question, but I can already guess the problem – she didn't mention anything about it in her Will, right?"

Laverty: "Right. Not a word about it, and she must have said it to me a thousand times, 'Irene, when I'm gone, I want you to have this cabinet.' Her Will was made out over fifteen years ago. She left everything to an old friend she hasn't seen in years. The woman doesn't want any of the property, she just wants it all sold and the money sent to her."

Counsellor: "Who is the executor?"

Laverty: "A trust company. They are going to auction the property off – convert it to cash. The cabinet will go."

Counsellor: "It's unfortunate, but so often true. People make promises that have no legal meaning once they die. They forget to change their Will, and there's nothing you can do about it, unless the beneficiary will make a gift of the cabinet to you."

Laverty: "I wrote and asked her, but she referred me to the trust company. She said she wanted nothing to do with the property settlement."

Counsellor: "Then, there's only one thing left to do. Attend the auction and buy the cabinet yourself. You will still retain some of the sentimental value that way."

Laverty: "It doesn't seem right. I know she wanted me to have the cabinet. She said so, so very often."

Counsellor: "But like many people, she didn't say so where it matters, in her Will."

Case Fifteen

Mr. and Mrs. H. Biggs entered the office, concerned with something about their new house.

Counsellor: "Are you the first owners?"

Mr. Biggs: "No, we bought the house from another couple. It is quite new and the house is fine. Our problem is outside."

Counsellor: "Go on."

Mrs. Biggs: "It's the landscaping. When we saw the house, it was just lovely in the yard. There must have been several hundred dollars in trees, bushes, roses, every imagineable plant placed just perfectly. But when we moved in, we found that the previous owners had dug most of them up and moved them. They filled in the holes, and re-seeded, but it isn't the same. Our problem is whether or not we bought those trees and plants when we bought the house."

Counsellor: "You certainly did. They had no right to take any of them."

Mr. Biggs: "When we asked them, they said that they had never promised to leave them in. They said that since they dug them up carefully, without tearing up the yard, they had the right to take them just like their furniture."

Counsellor: "No they did not. Standing trees and ornamental plants are part of the land and do not belong to anyone who is a tenant (tenant in this sense can mean owner) until they are lawfully cut for some reason. Digging up those trees and plants is unlawful conversion and you may order them returned."

Mr. Biggs: "What do we do?"

Counsellor: "Send them a registered letter demanding the return of all the trees and plants they removed. If they fail to do this within a reasonable period of time, you may sue and obtain a court order for either the return of your property or payment of a sum equal to the cost of having the plants replaced. You may also insist that they replant them, there is no obligation on you to do the work yourself."

Mr. Biggs: "Thanks. I thought we were right all along."

Counsellor: "The law of real property is complex, but generally anything attached to land is part of it. In this case, you were correct in determining that trees and bushes are part of the house and lot you purchased, whether any special mention was made or not."

Case Sixteen

Mr. R. Singh, of Malaysian birth, entered the office. During his years in Canada, he had developed his use of English to a fine degree. His business experience had not prospered so well.

Counsellor: "Mr. Singh, can we be of some service?"

Singh: "I am certain you may. I recently purchased from a private owner an appliance, an automatic washing machine, to be exact. I have encountered tremendous difficulties with the machine and would like to have the transaction reversed. In short, I want my money back."

Counsellor: "It's not all that easy. Tell me something about how you bought the machine."

Singh: "It was advertised in the newspaper as an automatic washer, excellent condition, owner must sell as he is moving into a small apartment. I visited the seller on two occasions. The machine was in good external condition. The owner said it was only two years old and never afforded him trouble."

Counsellor: "Did he actually say that?"

Singh: "No, but our conversation implied that. I asked if he had had any major troubles with it and he said no. He said he had used it for two years."

Counsellor: "Then he didn't say that at all. By saying he used it two years, he didn't even guarantee that he bought it new. His interpretation of what 'major trouble' is might be very different from yours."

Singh: "When I got it home, after paying $140 cash, I found that it kept blowing fuses. No matter what size of fuse I used, it blew them. I contacted an electrician and he said the machine was overloading. I contacted a repairman and he said the machine had serious trouble in the wiring. The motor probably needed to be re-wound and that would cost $35. I feel that I have a right to return this machine."

Counsellor: "I don't think so. Did you run the machine in the owner's house?"

Singh: "No, he did not offer to run it."

Counsellor: "Did you ask him to run it?"

Singh: "No. I did not see it run or try to run it until I got it to my house."

Counsellor: "Weren't you even curious to see if it did run?"

Singh: "I assumed he would tell me if it was not running. During my second visit, the basement had a lot of clothes drying on lines. I assumed they had been washed in that machine and the machine worked."

Counsellor: "Well, you see the problem here is that you cannot state if the machine worked or not before you moved it. If you attempt to blame the seller for anything wrong with the machine, he has several perfect defences against you. Firstly, he can claim that you damaged the machine while moving it. Secondly, he can fall back on the principle of 'buyer beware' and show that you inspected the machine twice, never asked to see it operated, and were obviously satisfied when you paid your money."

Singh: "I don't believe the machine was running when I bought it."

Counsellor: "But, never having asked to see it demonstrated, it is reasonable to assume that it did run at the time and that you have subsequently had a problem which is now your problem. The rule of 'caveat emptor' or, 'buyer beware' is a very old one. Basically, it says that the seller is not required to disclose to the buyer anything about the product which he knows would be detrimental to the sale. It is the duty of the buyer to satisfy himself before agreeing to buy. I can't understand why you would be satisfied without actually turning the machine on. I'm afraid a court would find that hard to understand as well. I believe you are stuck, Mr. Singh, caught by a very old principle of law that basically says a deal is a deal unless you can show genuine proof of misrepresentation or fraud, which I didn't find in any of the things you told me."

Singh: "It seems unjust."

Counsellor: "Perhaps, but it is not the duty of courts to make bargains for people. If you got a bad buy, then it should warn you to more caution in the future. If you don't know anything about horses, don't horse trade. If you don't know a good machine from a bad one, you should have taken an expert along with you to advise you. In future dealings, be sure to do that."

Case Seventeen

Mr. E. Watts, age 47, came into the office to discuss something he had received by mail.

Counsellor: "What sort of item?"

Watts: "Books, a whole set of them. I answered an ad that offered a free look at a set of nature books and received the first one. It said that if I wasn't pleased with the first one, I was entitled to keep it free, and would not be obligated to buy any."

Counsellor: "A reasonable trial offer, I'd say."

Watts: "Yes, and the first book was rather good, so I didn't say anything to them – didn't write or send a card, just kept the book. The next month they sent the second one, and I liked it, so I sent them $4.95 as indicated, to keep it. The deal was that I get a book each month, and could reject or accept any book, or send back the ones I didn't like. The second book wasn't all that good, and I thought the cost was a bit high. I still didn't write to them, thinking I would let matters drift a while."

Counsellor: "Then what?"

Watts: "They sent the entire set of books at once. I received a huge box with 18 books in it and a bill for $92.10 which they said covered handling. I never agreed to accept the entire set at once. I was thinking of cancelling my subscription if I ever had one. Do I have to pay for all those books?"

Counsellor: "If what you told me is correct, as it pertains to the nature of the agreement, then you do not have to pay for the books. I would suggest that you box the whole thing up, mark it 'Refused – Return to Sender' and send it back with the post office. In Ontario, a person who receives goods for which he did not ask, in the mail or by another method, may treat the goods as a gift and keep them. However, since you have already decided to pay for one book, this perhaps cannot be interpreted in that light. It is still a matter of contract that you do not have to accept something for which you have not bargained. Return them at their cost, or keep them boxed up, unused, and inform them by letter to come and pick them up. Also, advise them to send you no more books."

Case Eighteen

Mrs. T. Sheridan came into the office. Mr. Sheridan was not with her, in fact, he was her problem at the moment.

Counsellor: "Would you have a seat, and perhaps we can iron out your difficulty for you."

Sheridan: "I am separated from my husband at the moment. We don't have a separation agreement, he just deserted me. I have our two children. After he left, I got a job and we are managing fairly well."

Counsellor: "Are you seeking financial aid?"

Sheridan: "No. My problem is bills. When my husband left, we had tremendous bills, which he had run up in most circumstances, but some of them were just general bills for normal living. Those which I thought were extravagances of his, I ignored. For example, he financed a car. How he did it, I don't know, because he owed everyone in town, but amazingly enough he got this car. He never made a single payment, and when he left he took the car. They were after me for the money and I just told them there was no way I was going to be responsible for that car."

Counsellor: "Rightfully so."

Sheridan: "Other bills, which I thought were legitimate for myself and the children I tried to pay. These were things like charge accounts at department stores, and things bought with a credit card. I assumed the payments for these, even though they are all in my husband's name."

Counsellor: "Legally, you need not have done so, although it helps your credit standing in the community. You are stigmatized by his failure to attend to his credit payments."

Sheridan: "But I've found that I just can't keep up. The payments are taking much too much of my earnings and there are

	other things I need. Can I stop making those payments now that I have started making them, or do I have to see them through?"
Counsellor:	"First of all, a wife is not responsible for her husband's debts. She is a legally competent person and may contract and enter debts in her own name. Just because she is his wife, she is not automatically required to pay any bills he runs up in his own name. Were any of the charge accounts, credit cards, in your joint names?"
Sheridan:	"Just one."
Counsellor:	"That one you must pay. You are jointly responsible for it along with your husband. I would advise you to pay it up quickly and then cancel it, or your husband may still charge something else on it. All other debts, you may discontinue paying upon. Your previous payments do not bind you to full payment, they are only payments on your good faith to try to protect your own reputation and credit rating. Creditors cannot force from you any further payments since those are your husband's debts. Actually, since your husband deserted you, you could still charge more necessities to him. I would not advise that, though, unless you expect him to return to you some time."
Sheridan:	"No, I don't expect so."
Counsellor:	"Write to each creditor and advise them that you are separated from your husband and that you are not willing to be responsible for his debts. After that, you are starting afresh. You will find credit very difficult to obtain for yourself. His bad actions will injure you, and probably your children as far as credit ratings go. An unhappy situation, but nevertheless a real one."
Sheridan:	"Thank you so much. It will be much easier to be out from those bills."

Case Nineteen

Mr. E. Taulbee entered the office to discuss a problem he encountered with an appliance repairman.

Counsellor: "What was it you had repaired?"

Taulbee: "My television. It's a black and white, nineteen inch, and is only two years old. I took it into a shop and showed them the trouble I was having. I couldn't get one channel unless I twisted the dial around, pounded on it, etc. The man who took it in said the tuner was probably dirty and after the contact points were cleaned it would be all right."

Counsellor: "Did you sign anything?"

Taulbee: "I signed a work order. I asked them what it would probably cost and the fellow said it usually only runs a few dollars to clean a tuner. When I went back to get it, another man said the tuner was defective and they had replaced it for the amount of forty-seven dollars. I was really ticked off. I told them I wasn't paying that much when they said it would probably be only a few dollars."

Counsellor: "Do you have a copy of the work order?"

Taulbee: "No, I left the set there and walked out. The work order is still with it. I told them to put the old tuner back in and I'd be back for the set."

Counsellor: "You can't do that."

Taulbee: "Why not? I didn't agree to any forty-seven dollar bill."

Counsellor: "You did. When you signed the work order, I am willing to bet without even seeing it that you authorized the repairman to make whatever repairs were necessary to restore the set to working order. His guess that the tuner only needed cleaning turned out to be wrong. You can't hold him to that guess, because until he looked inside, he couldn't possibly know for sure. Having signed the work order, you freed him from his estimate and authorized him to make all necessary repairs. Now, he has a right of lien on that set. He can hold the set until you pay the forty-seven dollars. Failing to do that, he may sell the set to recover the parts and labour he put into it. I suggest you go and fork over the money and recover your set."

Taulbee: "That's robbery."

Counsellor: "No it isn't. A repairman can't see inside the set with some sort of magic X-ray eyes. You only asked him for a rough guess as to what might cause the problem. You did not ask him to prepare a precise estimate of repairs after he was inside the set. You did not tell him that you were limiting the amount of money you were willing to authorize for repair. You just signed a statement authorizing him to go ahead and fix it, which he did."

Taulbee: "But if I had known what it would cost . . . "

Counsellor: "You didn't know, and neither did he. As far as this matter is concerned, there is no further need of discussion, because you are in the wrong. I will tell you how to avoid similar problems in the future:

1. Advise the repairman to give you a full written estimate of necessary repairs. He cannot do this until after he has had a chance to get inside the set, so you will have to make two trips.

2. Having seen the written estimate, you may refuse to go ahead with any repairs because they are too costly. If you feel that some of the repairs are not absolutely necessary, then you can authorize in writing on the work order that you will not authorize repairs in excess of a certain amount. You have the right to limit in advance the extent of work you will permit and be responsible for.

In the present case, you gave the repairman full licence to do whatever he deemed necessary. He has done that, and now you must pay the amount."

Taulbee: "He's soaking me."

Counsellor:	"I couldn't say, because I am not a television expert. I would caution you not to repeat such statements to him, in front of his customers, or to third persons. If you do, he may sue you for slander. You could hurt his business reputation and be liable for that. In short, don't make allegations you cannot support. I should point out that if he tried to make you pay an absurd sum for the new tuner, such as $200 when they sell anywhere for $40 to $50, then you would have a right to refuse to pay what is called an 'unconscionable amount'. I don't think that is the case here."
Taulbee:	"You weren't much help."
Counsellor:	"In this case, perhaps not. In future cases, I hope I have helped you avoid trouble."

Case Twenty

Q. Lacey, age 35, was stuck.

Counsellor: "How so, Mr. Lacey?"

Lacey: "A #%¢&*()! bum cheque is how."

Counsellor: "Under what circumstances did it come to you?"

Lacey: "I sold a guy something and accepted his cheque as payment. It bounced. I called him and he just sort of said it was too bad . . . "

Counsellor: "Too bad?"

Lacey: "Yeah, he acted like I couldn't do nothing about it, now."

Counsellor: "Did he actually have an account in the bank upon which he drew the cheque?"

Lacey: "No. They sent it back to my bank with a piece of paper stapled to it saying they had no record of such account."

Counsellor: "What was the cheque for?"

Lacey: "I sold him my old power mower. It wasn't in very good shape, and I let it go for twenty dollars. He paid with a cheque and the cheque is phoney."

Counsellor: "Did you know the man?"

Lacey: "No, I never saw him before. I asked him for some identification and he showed me a driver's licence. I copied down the number, but it's him all right. When I called him on the phone, he didn't deny giving me the cheque, he just indicated that it was my tough luck."

Counsellor: "Well, it isn't. After the cheque bounced, how long did you wait before informing him the cheque was dishonoured?"

Lacey: "About five minutes."

Counsellor: "Fine. You must notify the drawer that his cheque was dishonoured within one business day, which you did.

Now, you can proceed against this man either by criminal or civil procedure, or by both. It is a criminal offence to write a cheque which the drawer knows in advance will bounce, particularly when the drawer knows he has no such bank account. This is a violation under Section 320 of the Criminal Code of Canada, a section dealing with obtaining credit by false pretence or false statement. Some people mistakenly believe that writing bad cheques is just a game. They assume that the victim will have to chase and hound them to get his money, and then he will just write another bad cheque to cover the first one. This is not the case, and it is a matter which Parliament recognized as serious enough to expand the Criminal Code to make it an offence punishable by up to two years in prison where the amount does not exceed fifty dollars. I suggest you inform him that you are going to bring a criminal charge against him unless the mower is returned immediately. If that doesn't faze him, bring the criminal charge. At the same time, file suit in Small Claims Court for the return of your property which the other man has no right to since he did not pay for it. You must ask the court for a Replevin Order to return your goods to you as lawful owner."

Lacey: "Isn't that expensive?"

Counsellor: "Not really. Small Claims Court is rather inexpensive and you may do the work yourself without hiring a lawyer. I would be surprised if it cost you more than $2.50."

Lacey: "Well, thanks . . . what was the section he can be charged with?"

Counsellor: "Section 320 of the Criminal Code. Writing bad cheques is not bad luck to the victim, it is bad luck to persons who still believe they can do it without punishment."

98

Case Twenty-One

Mrs. P. Millar entered the office with her daughter, Judy Millar.

Counsellor: "How can I help you?"

Mrs. Millar: "Well, it's about something Judy charged at a store. My husband and I have a charge account at several stores, including a large clothing store. We buy a considerable amount of clothing there for all the children, including Judy who is the eldest. Sometimes we let Judy shop for things by herself and put it on our charge account. But, we found out that she has been charging other things without our consent. The last bill I got was much too high, and when I asked the store where several items came from, they told me that Judy charged them. When I confronted Judy, she admitted it and said that she was keeping them hidden at a friend's house."

Counsellor: "Is that right, Judy?"

Judy Millar: "Yes, sir. They were really nice things, and my friend has some just like them. I kept them at her house so we could swap once in a while. We trade clothes all the time, and when my mother asked me where I got something, I just said it was my friend's. When her mother asked her where she got something, she said the same thing – that it was mine."

Counsellor: "I won't get into the moral aspect of it, since that is a matter you can deal with within the family circle. I'm sure Judy has been instructed that this was quite wrong for her to do."

Mrs. Millar: "She got that message clear, all right. But, she has over ninety dollars in clothes that I never permitted her to buy. I tried to take them back, but the store said they were used and would not give me a refund. I told them Judy had no consent from either her father or me to charge those things. The store manager said he didn't know that at the time, because we had allowed Judy to charge things in the past. Does that make a difference?"

Counsellor: "All the difference in the world. Having permitted Judy to use your charge account in the past, and having paid for what she bought, you have clearly indicated to the store that she has your permission to make purchases. Now, you must pay for what she bought. In the future, to avoid a recurrence, send them a letter that none of the children are to be allowed to make credit purchases. Or, better still, cancel the account."

Mrs. Millar: "I think I will cancel the account. They were really nasty about it."

Counsellor: "You had better have a long talk with the children about credit accounts. Now, in Ontario, they can start their own charge accounts when they reach the age of eighteen. Are they ready for that?"

Case Twenty-Two

Mr. C. Rodgers had a problem about something that had been stolen.

Counsellor: "Where was it stolen, Mr. Rodgers?"

Rodgers: "From my car. It was parked in front of the motel unit in which I was staying. The thief broke the window and stole several personal items in a bag and a small electronic calculator in a case."

Counsellor: "What legal question have you?"

Rodgers: "Well, my insurance company said my auto insurance policy would not cover such a thing."

Counsellor: "Usually not. Personal items are not considered part of the car, and it is the car that is insured against theft."

Rodgers: "But what about the motel? Don't they have an obligation to protect against their guests being robbed?"

Counsellor: "Not under the circumstances you mentioned. In Ontario, a motel comes under the Innkeepers Act, just like hotels do. The owner has an obligation to repay guests up to forty dollars for personal items stolen from your room, provided you kept the door locked and the room had a copy of the Innkeepers Act posted in a conspicuous place to advise guests they should put valuables in the office for safekeeping."

Rodgers: "This doesn't extend to a guest's car?"

Counsellor: "Afraid not. The owner can't insure that you lock your car, for example. I see no possible connection with him. Don't leave things in your car in plain sight, it attracts thieves who would otherwise leave it alone."

Case Twenty-Three

Mr. E. Robinson wanted to inquire about something his neighbour was pressing him into.

Counsellor: "What sort of deal?"

Robinson: "A loan. You see, he's kinda in trouble financially and he is trying to get a loan from a finance company. Now they said they would grant him the loan if he could get a cosigner. The way he explained it, a cosigner is just someone who tells the finance company that he is generally of good character, sort of a character reference."

Counsellor: "Hardly."

Robinson: "What is it then?"

Counsellor: "A cosigner is a person who promises to pay the debt if the borrower, the other signer, fails to pay it. What he is asking you to do is to take over his debt if he fails to pay it. If he is in trouble already, the chances are that he will fail to pay it, and you will be stuck. You would be safer to lend him the money yourself."

Robinson: "Well, he's not a dishonest guy, just a little goofy about dough. Spends it too fast, jumps from one thing to another, always borrowing somewhere."

Counsellor: "My advice can only be – forgot it. For one thing, there is nothing to kill a friendship faster than getting into a deal like this together. You're going to end up bugging him to make the payments on time, and he is quickly going to come to resent it. Secondly, he undoubtedly has had trouble making payments before or the finance company would not be looking for another signer. So, he could get laid off, get sick, be injured or killed on the job, and you are left with the whole debt. Frankly, I just can't see what's in it for you."

Robinson: "You know, neither can I. I think I'll tell him to find another pigeon."

Counsellor: "At least you won't regret it later."

Case Twenty-Four

W. Gage had a problem with property he loaned to someone.

Counsellor: "What sort of problem?"

Gage: "Well, I let a guy I work with borrow my boat last weekend. He took it fishing, trailer and all, and brought it back Sunday night. He didn't say anything, not even thanks. I found out Monday morning the reason why. There's a big rip down the side. I asked him about it at work and he said he "bumped" some rocks with the boat. I said he ran into them hard to make that hole. He really didn't want to say anything about it, so I asked him how he plans to make good the damage, and he just says that he's sorry about the hole, but that he doesn't have to pay me for the damage because I loaned it, not rented it. Is that right?"

Counsellor: "No, it isn't. Just because property is in the hands of another person on a gratis basis instead of a rental basis does not mean the borrower can wreck it and pay nothing. Lending property like this is called a bailment, and there are various kinds of bailments according to what the arrangement was. This bailment sounds like a bailment under which he, the borrower or bailee, received the sole benefit of the arrangement, since he did not pay you anything. Under this arrangement, he is required to take the greatest care of what he borrowed. This he failed to do by damaging your boat. He must make good the damage."

Gage: "What do I have to do?"

Counsellor: "Well, you could try getting him to understand his liability without getting difficult about it. Failing that, you will have to fix the boat and present him with a copy of the bill and demand payment. Lastly, you will have to sue to recover the amount. From what you have told me, you will have little trouble succeeding."

Case Twenty-Five

Mrs. W. Gilden had a problem with a television she bought from a stranger.

Counsellor:	"A bum set?"
Gilden:	"No, it works wonderfully. The trouble is that the person I bought it from did not own it."
Counsellor:	"Stolen or unpaid for?"
Gilden:	"Unpaid for."
Counsellor:	"What were the details?"
Gilden:	"It was advertised on the radio, on a tele-sale program. I heard it there and called the number. The man who answered said it was like new and he was only selling because he was moving out of the city and didn't want to pay to move a lot of things, including the T.V. I went right over and paid him seventy-five dollars for it. It's worth a lot more."
Counsellor:	"Then what happened?"
Gilden:	"I only had it a week, when a man called from a store and asked if I had it. I don't know how he knew I bought it, but he did, and told me that the set was not paid for. The man I bought it from had purchased the set under a conditional sales contract and there was still fifty dollars unpaid. He said I had to pay the other fifty dollars to keep the set. I called the man I bought it from, but he had moved away. Do I own the set or not?"
Counsellor:	"It depends upon one thing. Is the conditional sales contract registered at the court house? If it is registered, you do not own the set. You must pay the additional fifty dollars. If it is not registered, you own the set."
Gilden:	"How do I find this out?"

Counsellor: "Go to the court house and provide them with a description of the set including the serial number and inquire if the store has registered a conditional sales contract for that set. If the store has, then they remain the true owner and you must settle the amount with them. If not, you are the owner and the store can chase the man to whom they sold the set. I suspect that they were cautious enough to register it. That leaves you in the awkward position of trying to find the man who stuck you and recover your fifty dollars from him. You have a right to do so, if you can learn where he went.

Many people mistakenly assume that the person who is trying to sell them goods owns the goods. They forget that with so much buying on credit in our society there is a very good chance the goods are not the least bit paid for. In Ontario, if the name of the seller is plainly marked right on the goods, the seller does not even have to register the conditional sales contract. He remains the owner until all payments are made."

Gilden: "This is a brand name set, it doesn't have the store's name on it."

Counsellor: "Then, the answer lies in the court house. Either you own the set because the contract is not registered, or you do not own it because the contract is registered. Good luck . . . I'll keep my fingers crossed. In the future, check on the goods and their true owner before you buy."

Gilden: "It's terrible, you can't trust anyone these days."

Counsellor: "I know. Trusting people usually gets you into a legal jam, somewhere in life."